180
Morning
Devotions
for a
Joyful Heart

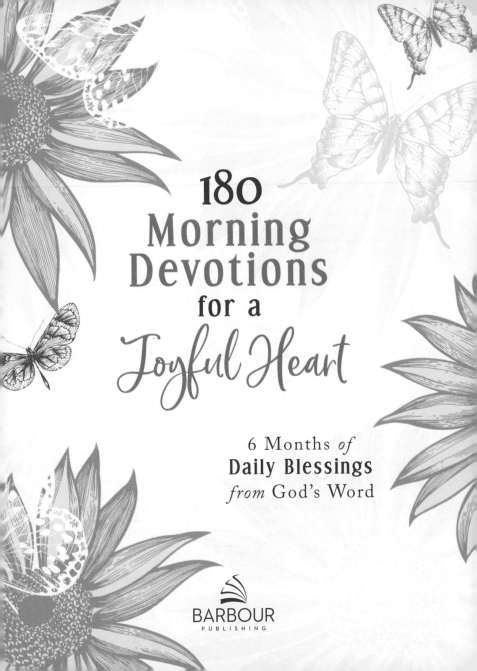

180
Morning
Devotions
for a
Joyful Heart

6 Months *of*
Daily Blessings
from God's Word

BARBOUR
PUBLISHING

Text previously appeared in *365 Morning Devotions for Women*, published by Barbour Publishing, Inc.

Scripture quotations marked niv are taken from the Holy Bible, New International Version®. niv®. Copyright © 1973, 1978, 1984, 2011 by Biblica, Inc.™ Used by permission. All rights reserved worldwide.

Scripture quotations marked nkjv are taken from the New King James Version®. Copyright © 1982 by Thomas Nelson, Inc. Used by permission. All rights reserved.

Scripture quotations marked nlt are taken from the *Holy Bible.* New Living Translation copyright© 1996, 2004, 2015 by Tyndale House Foundation. Used by permission of Tyndale House Publishers, Inc. Carol Stream, Illinois 60188. All rights reserved.

Scripture quotations marked msg are from *THE MESSAGE*. Copyright © by Eugene H. Peterson 1993, 1994, 1995, 1996, 2000, 2001, 2002. Used by permission of NavPress Publishing Group.

Scripture quotations marked kjv are taken from the King James Version of the Bible.

Scripture quotations marked ncv are taken from the New Century Version of the Bible, copyright © 2005 by Thomas Nelson, Inc. Used by permission. All rights reserved.

Scripture quotations marked nasb are taken from the New American Standard Bible, © 1960, 1962, 1963, 1968, 1971, 1972, 1973, 1975, 1977, 1995, 2020 by The Lockman Foundation. Used by permission.

Scripture quotations marked amp are taken from the Amplified® Bible, Copyright © 1954, 1958, 1962, 1964, 1965, 1987 by The Lockman Foundation. Used by permission.

Published by Barbour Publishing, Inc., 1810 Barbour Drive, Uhrichsville, Ohio 44683, www.barbourbooks.com

Our mission is to inspire the world with the life-changing message of the Bible.

Member of the
Evangelical Christian
Publishers Association

Printed in China.

Introduction

It seems like from the very moment we open our eyes we are on the go. We wake up, start the coffee, exercise, check emails, rush to work, eat breakfast, check our to-do lists…the tasks are endless! We fall into a routine after so many mornings, so by the time our alarm sounds, we barely think about what we have to do before our days begin.

But our morning can have a huge impact on how the rest of our day goes. No, we won't be able to know about every obstacle or plan for every circumstance. Instead, our morning gives us the chance to prepare our attitudes to face whatever happens. What better way to prepare than to spend time with God in prayer and in His Word?

This collection, meant for busy or laid-back mornings, focuses on truths that your heavenly Father wants you to know before you start your day. So grab that cup of coffee and that comfy chair (or maybe snuggle into bed just a little bit longer!) and make a little time in your routine to spend with the Lord.

Joy comes with the morning.
Psalm 30:5 nlt

Unfailing Love

Let your unfailing love surround us, LORD,
for our hope is in you alone.
PSALM 33:22 NLT

We hope that our sports team will win the big game and the local coffee shop will bring back our favorite order. We also hope that our jobs will continue to fulfill us and pay our bills and that God will answer a heartfelt prayer with a long-awaited yes.

Whatever we're hoping for, it's easy to think that God doesn't care about the details of our lives. However, God longs to share every part of our day. Why not talk to Him about all our needs and desires?

As we sip our morning coffee, we can jot down thanks for morning blessings such as flavored creamers and hot water for our shower. While we do our jobs, we can regularly bring our concerns (and coworkers) before God's throne. We could keep scriptures scribbled on sticky notes in our cubicle—or on our desk—to remind us to think with God's thoughts throughout the day instead of falling back on worldly patterns. When we lay our head on the pillow at night, we can voice the answered prayers which grace our lives, drifting off to sleep in gratitude at God's unfailing love.

Those small, simple actions add up to a day filled with hope and gratitude. . .and those days add up to a life well lived.

Father God, thank You for Your unfailing love.
Thinking on that love, which I haven't earned and can't repay,
causes me to fall to my knees in hope, gratitude, and joy.

Rejoicing!

Always be full of joy in the Lord. I say it again—rejoice!
PHILIPPIANS 4:4 NLT

Have you ever watched a toddler laugh? It's amazing, isn't it? Those adorable giggles are contagious. Before long you can't help but join in, your laughter filling the room. After all, nothing compares to the sheer joy of an innocent child. It bubbles up from the deepest God-given place, completely unhindered by concerns, worries, or distractions. How many times do we become so burdened by life's complexities that we forget to rejoice? What would it feel like to let those giggles rise to the surface, even on the worst days? What's that you say? You have nothing to feel joyful about? Look at those flowers blooming in the field! (Beauty!) Check out the food in your pantry. (Provision!) Glance into a grandchild's eyes or a coworker's heart. There's plenty of fodder for a joy-filled life. All we have to do is turn our focus from the pain to the glimpses of heaven right in front of us. Today, may your eyes be opened to many joy-filled moments.

*I'm grateful for this reminder, Father, that I can be filled
with joy, no matter the circumstances. They don't have
to drive my emotions. Instead, my joy can drive my
circumstances. Thank You for that reminder, Lord. Amen.*

Let God Reign!

Oh, how great are God's riches and wisdom and knowledge!
How impossible it is for us to understand his decisions
and his ways! For who can know the LORD's thoughts?
Who knows enough to give him advice? And who has
given him so much that he needs to pay it back?
For everything comes from him and exists by his power
and is intended for his glory. All glory to him forever! Amen.
ROMANS 11:33–36 NLT

It's easy for us to believe that we carry the world on our shoulders. We tend to believe, though we may not admit it, that we alone make the world turn. We convince ourselves that worry, finances, or power will put us in control. But in truth God is the one who controls all.

What a blessed peace awaits us! As you go about your day, rest in the assurance that God, not you, is in control. God understands every feeling you experience, and He can comfort you. God knows the best steps for you to take in life, and He is willing to guide you. He is above all and knows all, yet He is not out of reach.

Set your eyes firmly on the Lord, and He will care for you.

Lord, please let this truth sink deep into my heart today so that I may
live in joy and peace. Please guide me by Your wisdom and provide
for me according to Your riches. I praise You because You are good!

Don't Waste Your Talents

"His master replied, 'Well done, good and faithful servant!
You have been faithful with a few things; I will put you in
charge of many things. Come and share your master's happiness!'"
MATTHEW 25:23 NIV

Imagine inheriting a fortune and then burying the money in the backyard. You don't want to make a mistake in spending it, so you hide it. Most of us would agree this kind of thinking is ridiculous. We would spend the money, either putting it to good use or just for our pleasure.

The verse above is near the end of the parable of the talents. This servant used the talents the master had given him to create more talents. In biblical times a talent was a measure of weight used for precious metals. It was often used as money.

The spiritual gifts or "talents" God has given us are precious. Yet like a bar of gold sitting in a bank vault, they do no good unless they are used. Every believer receives spiritual gifts or "talents" after receiving Christ. The purpose of these gifts is to build up the Body of Christ.

When it comes to our spiritual gifts, many of us still have them buried in the backyard. We don't think we're good enough yet or we're afraid of making a mistake. But notice the servant didn't get judged on how well he did. Just on whether he used his talents.

Heavenly Father, give us the strength to step out and
use our talents without comparing ourselves with others.
Help us to glorify You in everything we do. Amen.

Beautiful for the King

*Before each young woman was taken to the [king]. . .
she was given the prescribed twelve months of beauty
treatments—six months with oil of myrrh, followed by
six months with special perfumes and ointments.*
ESTHER 2:12 NLT

Esther was just one of many women who had to take her turn at a full year of beauty treatments before being taken to the king. What a regimen!

Sometimes just one morning with cosmetics at the bathroom mirror can seem like forever, browsing through all the choices of creams, colors, and scents. Although it is enjoyable to have these products, some necessities, and maybe even a luxury or two, it's important to not focus more on our outward appearance than we should.

Our King does expect His children to take care of our bodies. After all, He created you. However, He doesn't expect everyone to be supermodels. Despite unrealistic beauty images on television and in magazines and movies impossible to live up to, all people are beautiful in the eyes of the one who created the whole earth.

Aren't you thankful that the King of kings doesn't require that you endure yearlong beauty treatments or be camera-ready for Him? He truly loves you just as you are—created in His image and loved beyond measure.

*Lord, help me not to place too much emphasis on
my outward appearance. Thank You for creating me
and for loving me just the way I am. Amen.*

The Alabaster Box

*As she stood behind him at his feet weeping, she began
to wet his feet with her tears. Then she wiped them with
her hair, kissed them and poured perfume on them.*
<small>LUKE 7:38 NIV</small>

The story of Mary and her alabaster box of high-priced perfume is a familiar one. Historically, this kind of perfume was given to a woman by her parents as a dowry. It was to be used on her wedding night, to be poured out on her husband's feet in an act of submission. So when Mary poured out this costly substance onto Jesus' feet, it was a statement of her complete love, devotion, submission, and obedience. She offered Him all of herself.

Many who witnessed the outpouring of this expensive perfume were angered because it could have been sold for a lot of money and used to fund ministry. They missed the point of her extravagant love. She took not cheap perfume but some of the most expensive ever made. And she didn't use just a few drops but emptied the container! Mary is a wonderful example for us—to love completely, being humbled at the feet of her Savior, and to offer her complete self. How beautiful and generous! May we be as well!

*Lord, I love You! May my love for You and Your people be
like a beautiful fragrance that leaves its essence everywhere
I go. I give myself wholly to You as You did for me. Amen.*

Giving out of Need

"Give, and you will receive. Your gift will return to you in full—pressed down, shaken together to make room for more, running over, and poured into your lap. The amount you give will determine the amount you get back."
LUKE 6:38 NLT

As usual, Jesus saw things from a different perspective. He was in the temple, watching people bring their gifts. Instead of honoring the Pharisees, with all their pomp and circumstance, Jesus points out a poor widow. "Truly I tell you," He said, "this poor widow has put in more than all the others. All these people gave their gifts out of their wealth; but she out of her poverty put in all she had to live on" (Luke 21:3–4 NIV).

While the rich gave out of their abundance, the widow gave out of her need. It's not difficult to give when we are sure all our needs are met. We just scrape a little off the top and leave it in the offering plate. Giving out of our poverty is a profound act of faith. When we lay our all on the altar, God promises to multiply it beyond our wildest imagination. What are you holding back from the Lord today? Give. God cannot wait to multiply your efforts.

Father, help me to be a giver. Teach me to give out of faith in You, not in my finances. Reveal to me where I may be holding back, waiting until my own needs for time or money are met. I long to trust You with the poor widow's faith. Amen.

When You Give Your Life Away

*Which of you, intending to build a tower, sitteth not down first,
and counteth the cost, whether he have sufficient to finish it?*
LUKE 14:28 KJV

Henry David Thoreau once said, "The price of anything is the amount of life you exchange for it." Busy lives often dictate that there is no time for the important things. People say, "Oh, I don't have time for this or that," or, "I wish I had the time. . ." The truth is you make the time for what you value most.

Every person has the same amount of life each day. What matters is how you spend it. It's easy to waste your day doing insignificant things—what many call time wasters—leaving little time for God. The most important things in life are eternal endeavors. Spending time in prayer to God for others. Giving your life to building a relationship with God by reading His Word and growing in faith. Sharing Christ with others and giving them the opportunity to know Him. These are the things that will last.

What are you spending your life on? What are you getting out of what you give yourself to each day?

*Heavenly Father, my life is full. I ask that You give me
wisdom and instruction to give my life to the things that
matter most. The time I have is precious and valuable.
Help me to invest it wisely in eternal things. Amen.*

Pride vs. Humility

A man's pride shall bring him low:
but honour shall uphold the humble in spirit.
PROVERBS 29:23 KJV

A great leader is known by his or her character. It is perhaps the things that one doesn't take part in that sets one apart. Great leaders are not prideful or boastful. They don't consider their accomplishments to be things they have done "in and of themselves," but they recognize the hand of God on their lives. Great leaders know that it takes a team to reach a goal. A great CEO treats the lowest man on the totem pole with as much dignity as he treats an equal. A great school principal knows that the teachers, assistants, bus drivers, and cafeteria workers make a huge impact on the students and the climate of the school. No one likes a bragger. It gets old hearing people go on and on about themselves. The Bible is filled with the teaching that the low shall be made higher and the proud will be brought to destruction. A paraphrase of this verse as found in *The Message* goes like this: "Pride lands you flat on your face; humility prepares you for honors." Take note of the areas of your own life where pride may sneak in and destroy. Replace pride with humility. Others will notice. You will not go unrewarded when you seek to be humble in spirit.

Father, root out any pride that You find in my
heart and replace it with humility, I ask. Amen.

God Is in the Details

Give all your worries and cares to God, for he cares about you.
1 PETER 5:7 NLT

Do you ever wonder if God cares about the details of your life?

Take a look at nature. God is definitely a God of details. Notice the various patterns, shapes, and sizes of animals. Their life cycles. The noises they make. Their natural defenses. Details!

Have you wandered through the woods? Towering trees. Their scents. The cool refreshment their shade provides. The different types of leaves and the tiny, life-bearing veins that run through them. How intricate!

What about the weather? It is filled with details from the hand of your God. The Creator sends raindrops—sometimes gentle and kind, other times harsh and pelting. He warms us with the sun, cools us with breezes, and yes—it is true—he fashions each snowflake, each unique, no two alike! The same way He designs His children!

Do you wonder if God cares about that struggle you are facing at work or the argument you had with a loved one? Is He aware of your desire to find that special someone or the difficulty you find in loving your husband? He cares. Tell him your concerns. He is not too busy to listen to the details. He wants to show Himself real and alive to you in such a way that you know it must be Him. The details of your life are not *little* to God. If they matter to you, they matter to God.

*Thank You, Lord, for caring about the details of my life.
It means so much to know You care. Amen.*

New Every Morning

*Because of the Lord's great love we are not
consumed, for his compassions never fail. They are
new every morning; great is your faithfulness.*
LAMENTATIONS 3:22–23 NIV

What's the first thing you do when you get up in the morning? Hop on the treadmill? Stumble to the kitchen for a mug of fresh-brewed caffeine? Walk blindly to the bathroom, not opening your eyes until a jet of hot water jolts you awake?

God starts out His day offering renewed compassion to His children. No matter what trials, difficulties, and sins yesterday brought, the morning ushers in a fresh experience, a brand-new beginning for believers who seek His forgiveness. All you have to do is accept the gift.

Are you burdened from yesterday's stress? Are the worries of tomorrow keeping you awake at night? Consider the dawning of the day as an opportunity to begin anew with our heavenly Father. Seek Him in the morning through studying His Word and through praying, embracing His compassion to be a blessing to others throughout your day.

*Father, Your promise of never-ending compassion for me is amazing!
I never want to take for granted the grace You offer every day.
I'm so undeserving, but still You give and give and give. Please help
me to show mercy to others the same way You do to me. Amen.*

Just in Time

As believers, our lives become exciting when we wait on God to direct our paths, because He knows what is best for us at any given moment. His plans and agenda are never wrong. We just need to practice living on His schedule and spending time in prayer. But that's easier said than done! Often we are chomping at the bit, and it's hard to wait.

Once we fully realize He knows best and turn our lives over to the Spirit for direction, we can allow God to be in charge of our calendar; His timing is what is paramount.

When chomping at the bit for a job offer or for a proposal, His timing might seem slow. "Hurry up, God!" we groan. But when we learn to patiently wait on His promises, we will see the plans He has for us are more than we dared hope—or dream. God promises to answer us; and it never fails to be just in time.

---

*Lord, I want Your perfect will in my life.
Help me learn to wait upon You. Amen.*

The Perfect Redeemer

"Who are you?" he asked. "I am your servant Ruth,"
she replied. "Spread the corner of your covering
over me, for you are my family redeemer."
RUTH 3:9 NLT

Ruth was a woman of faith. After suffering the loss of her husband, she could have wallowed in grief and misery. Instead, she chose to follow her mother-in-law, Naomi, to a place where she knew no one, in order to honor her late husband (and, perhaps, the God he had introduced her to).

Ruth was also a woman of action. She worked hard to glean in the fields, toiling with intention and consistency. The owner of the fields, Boaz, noticed her work ethic and was impressed. Later, Ruth followed Naomi's advice and found Boaz at night while he was sleeping. Because he was a relative of hers and a man of integrity, he agreed to spread his covering over her as her "family redeemer." This meant he promised to marry and take care of Ruth (and Naomi).

Ruth's story has much to teach us. Just as Ruth moved on from grief to action, we can ask for God's help to move past our own losses and not get stuck in bitterness or anger. With His help, we can honor others and not wallow in self-pity or destructive habits. Also, as His strength and forgiveness covers our weaknesses and failures, we can find peace and joy. He is the perfect Redeemer who takes care of us so we don't have to worry about providing for ourselves.

My rock and Redeemer, I praise and thank You for
Your covering over me. You are a faithful provider.

Ask for Joy

Rejoice the soul of Your servant,
for to You, O Lord, I lift up my soul.
PSALM 86:4 NKJV

The psalmist buried a nugget in this verse, showing us the source of joy and how to be joyful. All we have to do is ask, then look to God to "rejoice our soul."

So often we get stuck in frustration, depression, ingratitude, or anger. We go about our days feeling defeated, without the hope and joy the scriptures promise us. But have we asked our Lord for joy? Have we lifted our soul to Him?

Psalm 16:11 (NKJV) tells us, "In Your presence is fullness of joy." When we draw near to God, confessing our sin and our need of Him, we are met by His mercy, His forgiveness, His perfect love that casts out all fear. In the presence of that love, our joy is found, regardless of our circumstances. He is a father. He desires to love and care for His children.

Just as we want our children to come to us when they hurt, our heavenly Father longs to hear your voice crying out to Him. Sure, He already knows your need; but He also knows there is benefit for each of us in the confession, in crying out to Him. When we hear ourselves verbally lifting our souls to Him, we are reminded of our need of Him. Confession is good for the soul.

Father, help me to lift my soul to You, the source of joy.
Only You can make me to rejoice. Forgive my pride that
keeps me from confessing my sins. Draw me into Your
loving presence where there is fullness of joy.

What's in Your Heart?

Delight thyself also in the LORD: and he
shall give thee the desires of thine heart.
PSALM 37:4 KJV

What is it that you most desire? Is it a successful career or large bank account? Do you wish for someone with whom you can share romantic dinners or scenic bike rides? It really doesn't matter. What does matter is that you are fully committed to God. When that is the case, the desires in your heart will be the ones He places there. He will grant them because they honor Him.

Too many times we look at God's promises as some sort of magic formula. We fail to realize that His promises have more to do with our own relationship with Him. It begins with a heart's desire to live your life in a way that pleases God. Only then will fulfillment of His promises take place.

The promise in Psalm 37:4 isn't intended for personal gain—although that is sometimes a side benefit. It is meant to glorify God. God wants to give you the desires of your heart when they line up with His perfect plan. As you delight in Him, His desires will become your desires, and you will be greatly blessed.

Lord, I know You want to give me the desires of my heart.
Help me live in a way that makes this possible.

Equipped for the Task

[May God] equip you with everything good for doing his will, and may he work in us what is pleasing to him.
HEBREWS 13:21 NIV

God knew Paul the apostle would face hard times in his life. This distinguished, well-educated Pharisee went through an intensive training period for more than seven years, living obscurely in his hometown. God equipped Paul because He knew the price he would pay for following Christ: lashed five times, beaten three times with rods, stoned once, shipwrecked three times, adrift alone in the sea a night and day, robbed, rejected by his own countrymen, hungry, cold, naked, and resigned to a relentless thorn in his flesh. Through it all, many Gentiles came to know Jesus.

Hopefully, we aren't being equipped for a rigorous life like Paul's. But whatever He's called us to do, He will give what we need to accomplish it. You may not feel you are equipped, but God keeps His word. Scripture plainly states He's given you everything good for carrying out His work. When you are discouraged in ministry and you want to quit, remember He promises to work in you what pleases Him. The Spirit empowers us, making us competent for our tasks.

Lord, help me to draw on Your resources that I might be fully equipped for accomplishing Your tasks. Work in and through me to touch the lives of others as only You can do. Amen.

A Clear Focus

Hope deferred makes the heart sick,
but a longing fulfilled is a tree of life.
PROVERBS 13:12 NIV

We all have dreams and a desire to pursue them. But then life gets busy, and we become distracted with the choices we have to make on a daily basis. Do you go right or left, choose this way or that? Too much too fast is overwhelming, and looking for balance can leave us lost, not knowing which way to turn. The best way to gain your balance is to stop moving and refocus.

Jesus is your hope! He stands a short distance away, bidding you to take a walk on water—a step of faith toward Him. Disregarding the distractions can be hard, but the rough waters can become silent as you turn your eyes, your thoughts, and your emotions on Him.

You can tackle the tough things as you maintain your focus on Jesus. Let Him direct you over the rough waters of life, overcoming each obstacle one at a time. Don't look at the big picture in the midst of the storm, but focus on the one thing you can do at the moment to help your immediate situation—one step at a time.

Lord, help me not to concentrate on the distractions but to keep
my focus on which step to take next in order to reach You. Amen.

The Definition of Faith

*Now faith is confidence in what we hope for and assurance about
what we do not see. . . . And without faith it is impossible to
please God, because anyone who comes to him must believe that
he exists and that he rewards those who earnestly seek him.*

Hebrews 11:1, 6 niv

Eyes of faith help us see the spiritual gifts God gives us. Faith allows us
to see things normally unseen. Throughout the Old Testament, there are
stories of people whose faith in God demonstrates what faith in action
looks like: Abel sacrificed to God with a heart of worship, Enoch started
following God in his later years, Elisha saw angel armies, and Noah built
an ark in a land without rain.

In whom or what do you place your faith? God's character and His
promises are faithful. Faith is the pathway to our relationship with God.
We have faith to please God, to earnestly seek Him and believe in His
reward, even when we can't see it with earthly eyes. We need to cultivate
our eyes of faith, knowing that most of our reward for a faithful life will
not be found in this life but in the next.

How do you grow your faith? Start with obedience. Worship, walk
by faith, and share your journey with others. Faith will follow your obedience. Ask God to help you exercise your eyes of faith so you can see
Him working. If you can't see Him, ask Him to reveal Himself to you.

*Heavenly Father, thank You for making a relationship with
You possible. Help us to see You working in our lives. Amen.*

The Comparison Trap

But let each one examine his own work, and then
he will have rejoicing in himself alone, and not in
another. For each one shall bear his own load.
GALATIANS 6:4–5 NKJV

In John 21, the apostle John records a conversation Jesus had with Peter shortly after His resurrection. Jesus prepared a breakfast for His disciples after a night of fishing. Then Jesus invited Peter to go for a walk. Just days before, Peter had denied knowing Jesus. Now, three times Jesus asked Peter if the fisherman-turned-disciple loved Him. By asking this question, Jesus not only let Peter know that he was forgiven for his lapse of faith, but He also let Peter know that God still had a purpose and plan for Peter. He also spoke of how Peter would eventually die for His gospel.

Peter, maybe a little embarrassed by all the attention he was getting, looked over his shoulder and saw John following them. Peter asked the Lord, "What about him? How will he die?" Peter fell into the comparison trap.

Jesus answered, "What does it matter to you what I have planned for another? Live your life according to My plan. That's all you need to be concerned about."

And that's all Jesus still requires of His followers. God has a unique plan and purpose for each one, equipping them as they keep their eyes on Him and follow Him daily.

Father, show me Your plan for today and help
me not to compare my path with others. Amen.

The Spirit of Truth

*"If you love me, keep my commands. And I will ask the
Father, and he will give you another advocate to help you and
be with you forever—the Spirit of truth. The world cannot
accept him, because it neither sees him nor knows him. But
you know him, for he lives with you and will be in you."*

JOHN 14:15–17 NIV

Turn the other cheek. Love your enemies. Do good to those who hurt you. Give generously, Don't be anxious. Store up treasures in heaven. In the Sermon on the Mount (Matthew 5–6), Jesus presents a perspective on living that must have confused many of His listeners.

For those who don't know or recognize the Holy Spirit, Jesus' teachings don't make any sense. They are countercultural and go against the grain of natural instinct. When Christians are able to forgive those who have hurt them, give generously, or refuse to follow the latest trends and fashions, the world gets confused. To those who don't have the Holy Spirit, these seemingly extraordinary actions must seem unreal, impossible even. Knowing the Holy Spirit makes all the difference. When the Holy Spirit lives in us, we can finally see truth. We have the advocacy and the help we need to follow Jesus' commands—and they make all the sense in the world.

*Jesus, thank You for the gift of the Holy Spirit. My life would
be so meaningless and confusing without this precious comforter,
advocate, and friend. Help me to follow Your commands
and shine Your light to a watching world. Amen.*

I Am

*God said to Moses, "I AM WHO I AM. This is what you
are to say to the Israelites: 'I AM has sent me to you.'"*
EXODUS 3:14 NIV

The words "I am" ring out in the present tense. These words are used some seven hundred times in the Bible to describe God and Jesus. When Moses was on the mount and asked God who He was, a voice thundered, "I Am." In the New Testament, Jesus said of Himself, "I am the bread of life; I am the light of the world; I am the Good Shepherd; I am the way; I am the resurrection." Present tense. Words of hope and life. I Am.

Who is God to you today? Is He in the present tense? Living, loving, presiding over your life? Is the Lord of Lords "I Was" or "I've Never Been" to you? Have you experienced the hope which comes from an everlasting "I Am" Father? One who walks by you daily and will never let go? "I Am with you always."

We are surprised when we struggle in the world, yet hesitate to turn to our very Creator. He has the answers, and He will fill you with hope. Reach for Him today. Don't be uncertain. Know Him. For He is, after all, I Am.

---

*Father, we surrender our lives to You this day. We choose to
turn from our sins, reach for Your hand, and ask for Your
guidance. Thank You for Your loving kindness. Amen.*

Promises

*Let us hold firmly to the confession of our hope
without wavering, for He who promised is faithful.*
HEBREWS 10:23 NASB

In this life, you can have endurance and hope because your God is faithful to keep His promises. The Christian life would be hopeless if God were not faithful and trustworthy. But He will absolutely keep His promises. You can (and do) bet your life on that.

God has promised to complete and perfect the good work He has started in you (Philippians 1:6). He will never leave you or forsake you (Hebrews 13:5). He has promised that He will wipe away every tear from your eyes and that in heaven there will no longer be any mourning or crying or pain (Revelation 21:4). He will never allow you to be separated from His love (Romans 8:38–39). He promises that He will come again and that you will be with Him forever (1 Thessalonians 4:16–17). He assures you that no one can take you from His hand (John 10:29).

These are just some of the promises God has made. These aren't just nice sentiments. These are things that God will, without question, bring to pass. He does not break His promises—He will do what He has said He will do. You can put your hope in these promises, knowing that you won't be disappointed.

*Lord, in a world where promises are so often broken, thank You
that I can trust that You will keep Yours. What beautiful promises
You have made. I put my hope firmly in their fulfillment.*

Be Filled with Joy

Now the God of hope fill you with all joy and peace in believing,
that ye may abound in hope, through the power of the Holy Ghost.
ROMANS 15:13 KJV

Are you fighting a battle that seems futile? Have you lost hope of seeing a resolution? Take heart, you're not alone. Paul, the writer of today's verse, knew about battles, persecution, and rejection. He spent a lot of time writing his messages of hope while in jail. You may not be in a physical jail, but Satan may have you bound in a spiritual prison. It's time to break out of jail and be the victorious Christian you want to be. "How can I do that?" you ask. Look at what Paul wrote:

1. We serve a God of hope. Trust Him to supply you with hope to make it during dark days.

2. God is your source. Rely on Him to fill you with joy and give you peace in the time of trouble.

3. Believe that God is who He says He is, that He has made a way for you through His Son, Jesus.

4. Allow the Holy Ghost to empower you to abound in hope. We are often powerless to conquer our problems, but God's Spirit can arise within us to make us overcomers.

Push the darkness away. God is on your side. Allow Him to work for you.

Father, empower me by Your Spirit to abound in hope as You fill
me with Your joy and peace through the Holy Ghost. Amen.

Choosing Faith

Be still in the presence of the LORD, and wait patiently for him to act. Don't worry about evil people who prosper or fret about their wicked schemes. Stop being angry! Turn from your rage! Do not lose your temper—it only leads to harm. For the wicked will be destroyed, but those who trust in the LORD will possess the land.

PSALM 37:7–9 NLT

Our faith is tested when life doesn't go the way we expect it to, when people who aren't following God prosper, and we seem to be an afterthought. At times we even go so far as to blame God for the things that are going wrong.

Even though it seems like the wicked are prospering and we are sitting on the sidelines, our daily grind is not in vain. Each day we are faithful is another seed planted. It may take time for it to grow, but grow it will. There will be a harvest.

Faith sees the facts but trusts God anyway. Faith is forcing yourself to worry no longer but to pray in earnest and leave the situation in His hands. Faith is choosing to trust and rest in His plan, rather than fret about what could happen. We must choose faith even when we don't feel it. It is through choosing faith that we please God. Choose faith, and see what He will do.

Lord, despite what logic or the world tells me, I choose now to let my worries go and have faith in You. I trust that You will take care of every need, and I lay down all my burdens at Your feet.

Jesus' Perspective on Priorities

But Martha was distracted with all her preparations; and she came up to Him and said, "Lord, do You not care that my sister has left me to do the serving by myself? Then tell her to help me."
LUKE 10:40 NASB

We often wear busyness as a badge of honor because busyness can equal productivity and usefulness. It's important to ask ourselves, however, whether busyness takes away from—or adds to—our faith journey.

When Jesus dined in the home of Mary and Martha, Martha prepared the meal for her special guest, while Mary (in a highly unusual move for a woman during biblical times) sat at Jesus' feet, listening to His teaching. Martha understandably felt frustrated that Mary wasn't helping her, and she asked Jesus to rebuke her sister. However, Jesus told Martha that Mary had chosen the "better part." The Bible doesn't say what Martha replied, or how she felt. Perhaps she felt relieved.

Picture yourself receiving a text that an important person was coming to your house. You might scurry around, tidying the bathroom and plumping the couch cushions. If your guest said, "Sit down. Relax! I don't want you to make a fuss over me. I just want to be with you," you would feel grateful. . .peaceful. . .and treasured.

Today, as you plan your to-do list, prioritize time to sit and reflect on God's Word. Instead of rushing around to accomplish things you feel *should* be done, ask God what He wants you to do. You might be relieved.

*Jesus, give me Your perspective today as I plan my to-dos.
Show me what's important to You, and help me to follow through.*

God Is Good

Praise the LORD, for the LORD is good;
sing praises to His name, for it is pleasant.
PSALM 135:3 NKJV

We hear it in church. We say it to others. We want to believe it. God is good. All the time.

The Bible says it so we know it is true. Jesus lived it so we could see it in living color. But sometimes, when life yanks hard and pulls the rug out from under us, we begin to doubt. And that is probably a normal human temptation. Though we know that good parents discipline their children and sometimes allow them to learn "the hard way," we expect God, our heavenly Father, to do it differently.

So we need reminders. And He put them in our world everywhere we turn, at unexpected junctions and in the most ordinary places. Warm sunshine, brilliant flowers, rainbows after storms, newborn babies, friendships, families, food, air to breathe, pets, church dinners, sunrises, sunsets, beaches, forests, prairies, mountains, the moon and stars at night and puffy clouds in the day. All around us are hints that God is good and that His works are beautiful and life-giving.

When disease or tragedy or hardship enters our lives, we can rest assured that God is not the author of these destructive things and that someday He will cleanse this globe of its misery and set everything right. Until then, He has given us His strength, His hope, and His promise. That is enough to keep us going.

Father God, I praise You. You are good. Your works are
wonderful. I know You love me. Help me to trust Your
plan and purpose for me. In Jesus' name, amen.

Live in Unity

May God, who gives this patience and encouragement,
help you live in complete harmony with each other,
as is fitting for followers of Christ Jesus.
ROMANS 15:5 NLT

How does one live in unity with so many different types of people? One woman prefers vibrant, bold colors and has a personality to match. Another woman prefers muted tones, and her demure attitude fits accordingly. One church member might gravitate toward the classical, traditional hymns, while another prefers more contemporary music.

Christians disagree on a lot of issues, and conflicts often result—in and out of the Church. Yet we are to exercise the patience and encouragement God provides to help us live in harmony with one another.

One quotation says it well: "God prizes Christian unity above doctrinal exactitude." Our salvation is based on whom we worship, not where or how we worship. Quibbling over the cut, style, or color of our spiritual clothing causes us to succumb to our fleshly nature rather than God's will for us.

Personal preferences and heartfelt opinions are what make us individuals. Every believer has a gift to share within the Body of Christ. If we were all the same, how could we grow and learn? Jesus prayed for unity among the believers. God encourages us to do the same.

Father, thank You that You give me the ability and power
to walk in unity with my brothers and sisters in Christ.
I pray for Christian unity. Let it begin with me. Amen.

The Purpose of My Life

I long for your salvation, O LORD, and your law is my delight.
Let me live that I may praise you, and may your laws sustain me.
PSALM 119:174–175 NIV

We each have so many plans and goals and dreams for our lives, but our main mission should be to live each day to please God. Our purpose here on earth is to worship the God who created us and calls us His children.

Praise and worship isn't just about singing songs to God every Sunday morning. Praise and worship should be an everyday activity. Praise is about putting God first in our lives. It's about doing our daily tasks in a way that honors Him.

Can you really do laundry to please God? Can you really go to work to please God? Can you really pay the bills and make dinner to please God? The answer is a resounding *yes!* Doing all the mundane tasks of everyday life with gratitude and praise in your heart for all that He has done for you is living a life of praise. As you worship God through your day-to-day life, He makes clear His plans, goals, and dreams for you.

Dear Father, let me live my life to praise You.
Let that be my desire each day. Amen.

Wise Woman

*Then a wise woman cried out from the city, "Hear, hear!
Please say to Joab, 'Come nearby, that I may speak with
you.'. . . I am among the peaceable and faithful in Israel.
You seek to destroy a city and a mother in Israel."*

2 SAMUEL 20:16, 19 NKJV

In the midst of a siege on a city, the Lord sent an unlikely messenger to the commander of King David's army. A wise and courageous woman speaks into the chaos and preserves the city. She is Christ's calm in the storm, bringing reason into a tumultuous time.

We are called to be the calm in a storm. The only reason this woman could possibly speak with Joab amid the battle is through God's wisdom, power, and protection. She lays out the matter at hand before Joab and shows him his folly. She speaks the truth with grace and humility.

The same wisdom, power, and protection the Lord gave this wise woman He offers to you. In times of crisis, speaking and thinking rationally are difficult feats, but anchor your trust in the one and only unchanging God.

This woman did not demand; she did not provoke or diminish. She questioned Joab and asked for understanding. Our God is a God of understanding and wisdom, and though there are times He will not reveal the reason or purpose of an event, we must trust and rest in His unshakable character.

*Lord, may I stop and consider Your wisdom and Your
teachings when I face uncertainties. You are the only source
of wisdom; all my thoughts outside of You fail. Forgive
me for trusting in myself and not in You. Amen.*

Stand Still

*And Moses said unto the people, Fear ye not, stand still,
and see the salvation of the LORD, which he will shew to you to
day. . . . The LORD shall fight for you, and ye shall hold your peace.*
EXODUS 14:13–14 KJV

The children of Israel enjoyed a triumphant exodus from Egypt, but danger soon overtook them. They had only journeyed a short time when they looked up to see Pharaoh and his army marching toward them. They were afraid and immediately started making accusations against Moses, claiming he had brought them to the wilderness to die. They said they would have been better off staying in Egypt. But Moses encouraged them not to be afraid. They were to stand still. The Lord, their God, would fight for them. They were to hold their peace.

Are you facing an enemy? Do you feel afraid of impending danger? Moses told the people to do four things: fear not, stand still, see the salvation of the Lord, and hold your peace. The children of Israel experienced a great victory that day. God parted the waters of the Red Sea so they could cross over on dry ground, and then He allowed that same water to drown the Egyptian army. Moses' advice is good for us also. We can put our trust in God without fear and wait for God to do battle for us. Whatever is coming toward you, God can handle it.

*Lord, help me to stand still and wait for
You to work on my behalf. Amen.*

The Higher Road

"In this world you will have trouble.
But take heart! I have overcome the world."
JOHN 16:33 NIV

During World War II, the Nazis imprisoned author Dr. Viktor Frankl. As the Gestapo stripped him and cut away his wedding band, Frankl thought, *You can take away my wife, my children, and strip me of my clothes and freedom, but there is one thing you cannot take—my freedom to choose how I react to whatever happens to me.*

John 16:33 acknowledges that Jesus overcame the world on our behalf, so we are fully equipped to do the same.

It's difficult to trust God against all odds when problems slash us like a paper shredder. Yet it is during those times that God gives us a clear choice: choose faith or break under the harsh realities of life.

Dr. Frankl had learned somewhere in his life's journey to take the higher road. He knew that faith and how we react to people or problems is a choice, not a feeling. We can respond in the flesh or submit to the Holy Spirit whatever happens to us. Often that means asking for forgiveness though you've done nothing wrong, encouraging someone despite their negative attitude, or extending a hand and risking rejection.

Mature believers know that hardships are a part of life, but Jesus has paved the pathway to overcome. And although taking "the higher road" is less traveled, it's worth the trek.

Lord, whatever I face, may I act, not react,
with Your overcoming power. Amen.

No Matter What

Be thankful in all circumstances, for this is
God's will for you who belong to Christ Jesus.
1 Thessalonians 5:18 NLT

Sometimes being thankful seems almost impossible. How can I be thankful when I'm working as hard as I can and I'm still unable to pay off all my debt? How can I be thankful when my car dies, my water pump breaks, or my wallet is stolen? How can I be thankful when my parents split up or my boyfriend breaks my heart or my children refuse to behave?

Living in today's world is difficult, and we often experience hardships that make being thankful extremely difficult. When Paul wrote this verse, however, you can bet that he did not write it lightly. He knew what it was to experience hardships and suffering. But Paul also knew the wonderful power and blessing that comes from having a relationship with Christ.

Jesus enables us to be thankful, and Jesus is the cause of our thankfulness. *No matter what happens,* we know that Jesus has given up His life to save ours. He has sacrificed Himself on the cross so that we may live life to the fullest. And while "to the fullest" means that we will experience pain as well as joy, we must *always* be thankful—regardless of our circumstances—for the love that we experience in Christ Jesus.

Dear Lord, thank You for Your love. Please let
me be thankful, even in the midst of hardships.
You have blessed me beyond measure. Amen.

Abide in the Vine

*"I am the vine; you are the branches. If a man
remains in me and I in him, he will bear much
fruit; apart from me you can do nothing."*
JOHN 15:5 NIV

Fruit is the tangible evidence of life. Only live plants can produce fruit. Nourishment travels from the roots to the branches, sustaining the fruit. Jesus refers to Himself as the vine and to us as branches. Unless we are attached to the vine, we are not receiving spiritual nourishment. We become grafted into the vine by faith in Jesus Christ as Lord and Savior. His power then flows through us, producing spiritual fruit.

The fruit we bear is consistent with His character. Just as apple trees bear apples, we bear spiritual fruit that reflects Him. Spiritual fruit consists of God's qualities: love, joy, peace, patience, kindness, goodness, faithfulness, gentleness, and self-control. The fruit of the Spirit cannot be grown by our own efforts. We must remain in the vine.

How do we abide in Him? We acknowledge that our spiritual sustenance comes from the Lord. We spend time with Him. We seek His will and wisdom. We are obedient and follow where He leads. When we remain attached to Him, spiritual fruit will be the evidence of His life within us. Abide in the vine and be fruitful!

*Dear Lord, help me abide in You so that I may produce
fruit as a witness to Your life within me. Amen.*

God Cares for You

*"Consider how the lilies grow. They do not labor or spin. Yet I
tell you, not even Solomon in all his splendor was dressed like
one of these. If that is how God clothes the grass of the field,
which is here today, and tomorrow is thrown into the fire,
how much more will he clothe you, O you of little faith!"*
LUKE 12:27–28 NIV

Take a look at God's creation. He has created this world with such intricate
detail. He designed every tree, the majestic mountains, a glorious sun, and
a mysterious moon. Each animal has been given unique markings, parts,
and sounds. Consider the long-necked giraffe, the massive elephant, the
graceful swan, and the perfectly striped zebra!

If God makes the flowers, each type unique and beautiful, and if
He sends the rain and sun to meet their needs, then will He not care
for you as well?

He made you. What the Father makes, He loves. And that which
He loves, He cares for. We were made in His image. Humans are dearer
to God than any of His other creations. Rest in Him. Trust Him. Just
as He cares for the birds of the air and the flowers of the meadows, God
is in the business of taking care of His sons and daughters. Let Him
take care of you.

*Father, I am amazed by Your creation. Remind me that I am Your
treasured child. Take care of me today as only You can do. Amen.*

Look Up!

Your love, LORD, reaches to the heavens,
your faithfulness to the skies.
PSALM 36:5 NIV

In Bible times, people often studied the sky. Looking up at the heavens reminded them of God and His mighty wonders. A rainbow was God's sign to Noah that a flood would never again destroy the earth. God used a myriad of stars to foretell Abraham's abundant family, and a single star heralded Christ's birth.

The theme of the heavens traverses the scriptures from beginning to end. The Bible's first words say: "In the beginning God created the heavens" (Genesis 1:1 NIV). The psalmist David shows God's greatness in comparison to them: "the heavens declare the glory of God" (Psalm 19:1 NIV). And in the New Testament, Jesus describes the end times, saying, "There will be signs in the sun, moon and stars. . . . At that time [people] will see the Son of Man coming in a cloud with power and great glory" (Luke 21:25, 27 NIV).

Some of God's greatest works have happened in the sky.

This immense space that we call "sky" is a reflection of God's infinite love and faithfulness. It reaches far beyond what one can see or imagine, all the way to heaven. Too often, working, maintaining households, parenting, and doing other tasks keep us from looking up. So take time today. Look up at the heavens and thank God for His endless love.

Heavenly Father, remind me to stop and appreciate
Your wonderful creations. And as I look upward,
fill me with Your infinite love. Amen.

Move the Stone

"Roll the stone aside," Jesus told them. But Martha,
the dead man's sister, protested, "Lord, he has been
dead for four days. The smell will be terrible."
JOHN 11:39 NLT

Jesus had been a frequent visitor to Martha's home. Now He has come again to raise her brother from the dead. Though, if you asked Martha, if Jesus had come when they first asked Him to, her brother wouldn't be dead. And now He wants to open up the tomb. Martha doesn't understand any of it.

When Jesus asks for the tomb to be opened, Martha doesn't express amazement that Jesus intends to raise her brother from the dead. Instead, she's worried about the smell.

Aren't we often like that? God tells us to do something, to take a step of faith, to do our part so He can work. Instead of focusing on what God's going to do, we worry about how it's going to affect us.

It's also interesting that Jesus asked for the stone to be moved. If He was about to resurrect a dead body, moving a stone from in front of the tomb was a small thing. But He wanted their participation. He wanted them to put their faith in action. If they believed He was really going to raise a body that had been dead four days, then moving the stone from the tomb was the first step to show their faith.

Dear Lord, show us where we need to step out in faith, and give us
the courage to do it. Help us to trust You with everything. Amen.

The Gift of Prayer

First of all, then, I urge that entreaties and prayers,
petitions and thanksgivings, be made on behalf of all men...
This is good and acceptable in the sight of God our Savior.
1 TIMOTHY 2:1, 3 NASB

There is such joy in giving gifts. Seeing the delight on someone's face to receive something unexpected is exciting. Perhaps the absolute greatest gift one person can give to another doesn't come in a box. It can't be wrapped or presented formally, but instead it is the words spoken to God for someone—the gift of prayer.

When we pray for others, we ask God to intervene and to make Himself known to them. We can pray for God's plan and purpose in their lives. We can ask God to bless them or protect them. You can share with them that you are praying for them or do it privately without their knowledge. Who would God have you give the gift of prayer to today?

Lord, thank You for bringing people to my heart and mind
who need prayer. Help me to pray the things that they need
from You in their lives. Show me how to give the gift of
prayer to those You would have me pray for. Amen.

Seek Him

David understood what it takes to dwell with God. He continually gazed at His beauty. At the time he composed this psalm, David was living on the run, not in the lavish palace of a king. He was finding beauty and richness in the starkest of environments, stripped of amenities.

Do we seek God's beauty in our environment, which is not quite so bleak? Isn't His beauty reflected in the smiling toddler in the grocery store line? What about the elderly married couple's hand-holding throughout the church service? Don't these reflect our Creator?

When we bite into an apple—crisp, sweet, and naturally packaged for freshness—or observe the grace and agility of a dancer or listen to the intoxicating notes of a flute, don't they reveal more about God? Where did it all originate? Whose power and creativity is behind it all? Life reveals glimpses of His power and awesomeness. These everyday things draw us into His presence where we can praise Him, enjoying His beauty and greatness all the days of our life.

Magnificent Creator, Your greatness and beauty surround me. May my eyes gaze at You, seeking You, that I might dwell in Your presence continually. Amen.

Cultivating Contentment

*I wait for the LORD, my soul waits, and in his word I put
my hope. I wait for the Lord more than watchmen wait for
the morning, more than watchmen wait for the morning.*
PSALM 130:5–6 NIV

What are you waiting for—a job, a relationship, physical healing, financial provision? Whatever answer to prayer you are longing for, remember that often it's in the waiting that God performs His perfecting work on our character. Joseph waited for many years, serving in Pharaoh's house (even ending up in jail) before God promoted Him. Abraham waited until he was a century old to see the child God had promised to him and Sarah decades before. God was still at work in both men's lives, though His actions and plans were hidden.

Maybe you've waited for God to come through, and so far, He hasn't. The word *advent* means "arrival or coming, especially one which is awaited." Like the silence the people of Israel endured for 400 years between the last spoken prophetic word and the arrival of the Christ child, perhaps you've endured silence from God for so long that you think He's not there, not listening—or not inclined to come to your rescue.

No matter what you're going through, please know that God is for you, not against you. He aches with you. And He offers us a choice: be chained in fear or changed by grace.

Which will you choose today?

*Father, forgive me for doubting Your love and mercy.
Thank You that You are faithful and that You will
provide for me. I believe. . .help my unbelief.*

True Friendship

Rejoice with those who rejoice;
mourn with those who mourn.
ROMANS 12:15 NIV

True Christian friendship has this verse stamped all over it. Do you have a friend who truly finds joy in your successes? When you are on top of the world, this person is genuinely happy for you. When you are sad, you have seen tears come to her eyes. This is not a friendship found every day. It is rare and to be treasured.

As believers in Christ, we have this high call on our lives. Pray that you might truly celebrate with others, not be secretly wishing you were the one receiving the blessing. On the other hand, know that at times sorrow and loss is so deep that a hug and an "I love you" will mean the world. Lots of words are not needed in such times. To mourn with the mourner is the greatest gift you can give. Just to show up, to extend help, to show love.

If you have such a friend, you no doubt cherish her. Make it your aim to live out Romans 12:15 in small ways this week. Stand and cheer when others are victorious. Stand close by and be ready to comfort them when they experience disappointment or loss.

Heavenly Father, help me to rejoice with those who
rejoice and to mourn with those who mourn. Give me
a sensitive heart that is focused on others. Amen.

A Friend Who Sticks
Closer than a Brother

*Now it came about when he had finished speaking
to Saul, that the soul of Jonathan was knit to the
soul of David, and Jonathan loved him as himself.*

1 SAMUEL 18:1 NASB

The relationship between David and Jonathan was like that of brothers. Proverbs 18:24 (NIV) says it this way: "One who has unreliable friends soon comes to ruin, but there is a friend who sticks closer than a brother." Everyone hits a rough patch now and then. This world is not our home. As believers, we are aliens here. One day we will truly be at home in heaven with the Lord. Until then, it is important that we stand strong with one another through the ups and downs of life. Consider the depth of Jonathan's love for David:

Jonathan, the son of King Saul, protected David from death when Saul grew jealous of David. He created a secret way of getting the message to David that he indeed needed to flee the kingdom. The two hated to part, but it was their only option. In the end, the Bible tells us it was David who wept the hardest when he had to leave Jonathan. No doubt, David recognized the value of his true friend who stuck closer than a brother. Do you have a friend in need? Life gets busy. Don't ever be too busy to help your friends, to be there for them as Jonathan was for David.

*Father in heaven, may I be a friend who
truly sticks closer than a brother. Amen.*

Setting Priorities

Cause me to hear Your lovingkindness in the morning,
for in You do I trust; cause me to know the way in
which I should walk, for I lift up my soul to You.
PSALM 143:8 NKJV

We twenty-first-century women have more choices than any other generation before us about what we do with our time. How easy it is to overcommit ourselves, become stressed, and let our lives get out of balance. We have work, sleep, relationships, recreation, and responsibilities of every sort vying for our time.

Twenty-four hours. That's what we all get in a day. Though we often think we don't have time for all we want to do, our Creator deemed twenty-four-hour days sufficient. How do we decide what to devote ourselves to? The wisdom of the psalmist tells us to begin the day by asking to hear the loving voice of the one who made us. We can lay our choices, problems, and conflicts before Him in prayer. He will show us which way to go. Psalm 118:7 (NIV) says, "The LORD is with me; he is my helper." Hold up that full plate of your life to Him, and allow Him to decide what to keep and what to let go.

Lord, make me willing to surrender my choices and activities
to You. Cause me to desire the things You want me to do.

God Is Bigger Than the Wrong Done to You

"But if you do not forgive others their sins,
your Father will not forgive your sins."
MATTHEW 6:15 NIV

It can be tough to forgive. It presses us to the edge of ourselves where we are forced to acknowledge that God is greater than the wrong that has been done to us. When we choose to forgive, it keeps God's power in perspective.

Someone may stop loving you, insult you, steal from you, or abuse you, but that person will never be able to destroy the love that God has for you or His sovereign rule over all that concerns you. God's redeeming love is bigger than your enemies. This is what Joseph acknowledged after his brothers threw him into a pit and sold him into slavery: "You intended to harm me, but God intended it for good" (Genesis 50:20 NIV).

Think about something someone has done to you that has demanded forgiveness. Do you believe God is bigger than the wrong? Are you convinced His love and His rule are redemptive? If so, let the person who has wronged you off the hook. Stop thinking that he or she has ruined your life and that you will never recover—because God is a redeemer.

Lord, when someone wrongs me, I may want to lash out or hold
a grudge. Help me to remember that there is nothing that will
happen to me that You cannot redeem for my good and Your
glory. Help me to live in the freedom of this truth. Amen.

Thank You, Lord

I will praise the LORD at all times;
I will constantly speak his praises.
PSALM 34:1 NLT

While imprisoned, the apostle Paul gave thanks to God, even singing His praises, and it resulted in the salvation of the jailer and his household. What a great lesson for every Christian—when you feel least like giving thanks, that's precisely when you should!

What is your response when you find yourself trapped in traffic, late for a meeting, frustrated in your plans, sick in bed, hurting emotionally, overwhelmed with work, lonely, tired, or confused? Our human nature teaches us we should gripe and fret. Yet scripture says we should give thanks. Only when we surrender our lives to Him and His control is this possible.

Learn to thank Him. Thank Him for being your help in time of trouble. Thank Him for His great wisdom and power. And thank Him for causing every situation in your life to work together for your good.

Giving thanks may not change your circumstances significantly, but it will change you. You'll feel yourself focusing on God—His goodness, kindness, and grace—rather than your own anger, pride, sickness, or inconvenience. Maybe that's why it's such fertile soil for miracles. The biblical commentator Matthew Henry stated it well: "Thanksgiving is good, but thanks-living is better."

Lord, I choose to give You thanks today for whatever comes my way.
I love You, Lord, and I am grateful for Your goodness. Amen.

A Joyful Noise

Sing aloud unto God our strength:
make a joyful noise unto the God of Jacob.
PSALM 81:1 KJV

Aren't you glad the Bible commands us to "make a joyful noise" unto the Lord instead of saying something like "Sing like an angel"? Many are born with amazing vocal abilities. They wow us with their choir productions and their amazing solo performances. But some of the rest of us are lucky to croak out a word or two in the right key.

God doesn't care about your vocal abilities. He longs to hear a song of praise rise up out of your heart, even if it's sung in three or four keys. Think about that for a moment. He's listening as millions of believers sing out—in every language, every key, every pitch. And it doesn't bother Him one bit because He's not listening to the technique, He's listening to the heart.

Still not convinced? Read the book of Psalms from start to finish. It will stir up a song in your heart, and before long your toes will be tapping and your heart bursting. Why? Because you were created to praise Him. So don't worry about what others will think. Make a joyful noise!

Lord, my heart wants to sing happy songs today! I'm not
going to worry anymore about my voice, whether I'm
singing in church or in the car or in the shower. I was made
to praise You, Father, so I choose to make a joyful noise!

Comfort in Sadness

You've kept track of my every toss and turn
through the sleepless nights, each tear entered in
your ledger, each ache written in your book.
PSALM 56:8 MSG

In heaven there will be no more sadness. Tears will be a thing of the past. For now, we live in a fallen world. There are heartaches and disappointments. Some of us are more prone to crying than others, but all of us have cause to weep at times.

Call out to God when you find yourself tossing and turning at night or when tears drench your pillow. He is a God who sees, a God who knows. He is your "Abba" Father, your daddy.

It hurts the Father's heart when you cry, but He sees the big picture. God knows that gut-wrenching trials create perseverance in His beloved daughter and that perseverance results in strong character.

Do you ever wonder if God has forgotten you and left you to fend for yourself? Rest assured that He has not left you even for one moment. He is your Good Shepherd, and you are His lamb. When you go astray, He spends every day and every night calling after you. If you are a believer, then you know your Good Shepherd's voice.

Shhhh. . .listen. . .He is whispering a message of comfort even now.

Father, remind me that You are a God who sees my pain.
Jesus, I thank You that You gave up Your life for me. Holy
Spirit, comfort me in my times of deep sadness. Amen.

A Creative God

In the beginning God created the heavens and the earth.
<small>GENESIS 1:1 NIV</small>

Did you realize that you are made (designed, created) in the image of a very creative God? It's true! He breathed life into you, after all. It stands to reason that some of His creativity would have spilled over into you, His daughter.

The same God who created the heavens and the earth—who decided a giraffe's neck should be several feet long and a penguin should waddle around in tuxedo-like attire—designed you, inside and out! And He gifted you with a variety of gifts and abilities, all of which can be used to His glory.

So what creative gifts reside inside you? Have you given them a stir lately? Maybe it's time to ask God which gifts are most usable for this season of your life. He's creative enough to stir the ones that can be used to reach others. He will bring them to the surface and prepare you to use them—much like He did during Creation—to bring beauty out of dark places.

So brace yourself! Your very creative God has big things planned for you!

Lord, thank You for creating me in Your image. I get so excited when I think about the fact that Your creativity lives inside me. Just as Your Spirit moved across creation in the book of Genesis, I ask You to move across the creative gifts in my life and stir them to life!

Use It or Lose It

"Therefore consider carefully how you listen."
LUKE 8:18 NIV

Doing God's Word, not merely hearing it, was one of Jesus' repeated themes. His parable of the sower illustrated four different responses we can have whenever the seed of the Word of God hits our thinking. With a hard heart, we will have no response and the truth will disappear as if *stolen*. A rocky heart *starves* the seed, not allowing it to take root. If our heart is cluttered with weeds of worldly cares, the seed gets *strangled*. But with a positive response to truth, we *sustain* it and let it change us, producing fruit in our lives.

Jesus concluded by saying that the more truth we learn and practice, the more God will reveal. But if we stop using what we learn, we will lose even what we thought we had (Matthew 13:12; Mark 4:24–25; Luke 8:18). If we do nothing with the seed, it can do nothing for us.

This principle reminds me to evaluate what I do with truth from God. When I read His Word or hear a sermon, do I respond to Him obediently? Does it correct my behavior, shape my worldview, and get all the way to my fingers and feet? Like panning for gold, the more I seek, the more I will discover. James 1:25 says that continuing in God's Word—not forgetting what we hear, but doing it—makes us blessed in what we do.

Perfect Father, every time I encounter Your Word,
help me to respond positively and use it so that
Your truth will grow and bear fruit in me.

Love Leads the Way

You have seen what I did to the Egyptians, and how I
carried you on eagles' wings, and brought you to Myself.
EXODUS 19:4 AMP

When Moses led the children of Israel out of Egypt toward the Promised Land, he did not take them on the shortest route. God directed him to go the long way lest the people turn back quickly when things became difficult. God led them by day with a pillar of clouds and by night with a pillar of fire. How clearly He showed Himself. The people placed their hope in an almighty God and followed His lead. When they thirsted, God gave water. When they hungered, He sent manna. No need was unmet.

The amount of food and water required for the group is unimaginable. Moses depended upon God. He believed God would care for them. Because he knew of God's great love and trusted in the Creator.

If God can do this for so many, do you not think He will care for you? He knows your needs before you even ask. Place your hope and trust in Him. He is able. He's proven himself over and over. By reading the scriptures and praying to the one who loves you, you can feel His care is infinite. His word is final. God loves you.

Lord, help me see You gave Your life for me.
Teach me to trust in You. Amen.

Forgiveness

But Esau ran to meet Jacob and embraced him;
he threw his arms around his neck and
kissed him. And they wept.
GENESIS 33:4 NIV

Jacob cheated Esau out of his birthright and the father's blessing reserved for the eldest son. Jacob's act changed both their lives forever. Esau hated Jacob for his deception and betrayal. His anger ran so deep that he planned to kill Jacob, and he would have had Jacob not fled for his life. Jacob stayed away for twenty years and then started for home even though he feared Esau. What a surprise when Esau ran to meet him and threw his arms around Jacob. He had forgiven Jacob even though his betrayal had been a cruel one.

Forgiveness isn't always easy. Sometimes the hurt is deep and the pain lingers for a long time. The other person seems to get on with her life while you suffer. Esau could have hung on to his anger and killed Jacob when he saw him coming. Instead, he took the first step and ran to meet Jacob, forgiving him. We too can take the first step toward forgiveness. In doing so, we let go of the pain we've been carrying. We find freedom for ourselves and offer the same to the one who hurt us. Is there someone you need to forgive today? Take the first step toward reconciliation. God will give you the strength to go the full distance.

Lord, give me courage to take the first step toward
forgiveness even if it's the other person's fault. Amen.

Draw Near with Confidence

*Therefore let us draw near with confidence to the throne of grace,
so that we may receive mercy and find grace to help in time of need.*
HEBREWS 4:16 NASB

In this verse you are told that you can approach God's throne with confidence. Why do you approach the throne? So that you can "receive mercy and find grace to help in time of need." Why would you need to receive mercy? Those who need mercy are those who have done something wrong, those who are not in right standing with whomever they are asking mercy from. Inevitably you come before the throne of God with the baggage of your sin. And yet you are told to come with confidence before the throne of a holy God who hates sin. You don't need to be perfect or have your act together to come before God with confidence. You only need to be covered in Christ's blood. This confidence with which you approach God's throne is not a self-confidence, but a God-confidence. It's a confidence that assures you that God is for you, that He loves you, and that He sees Christ in you. Your standing before God depends completely on His view of you and not on your own merit. And He sees you as His beloved child. So go boldly to the foot of His throne, knowing that you will receive mercy and grace.

*Lord, thank You that I don't need to be perfect before
I can come before You. I come before You now with
my confidence placed in You, not in my own merit.*

A Touch of Faith

Jesus turning and seeing her said, "Daughter, take courage; your faith has made you well." At once the woman was made well.
MATTHEW 9:22 NASB

There once was a woman who'd been hemorrhaging for twelve years. She sought help from a myriad of physicians and spent all that she had, but her issue of blood was worse than ever before. Then one day she heard a healer named Jesus was coming to town. Although she was considered the lowest of the low, someone who shouldn't even be out in public, she decided to make her way through the crowd and reach out to this Man. Risking all she had left, she came up behind Him and touched His garment, for she kept saying to herself, "If I can just touch his robe, I will be healed" (Mark 5:28 NLT). Instantly her bleeding stopped. But the story doesn't end there. Jesus immediately felt power flowing out of Him and demanded, "Who touched me?" (Mark 5:31 NLT). Shaking with fear, the woman confessed it had been her. Jesus responded with tenderness and encouragement, "Daughter, your faith has made you well. Go in peace. Your suffering is over" (Mark 5:34 NLT).

What issue have you needed Jesus' help with? What desperately bold exchange between your soul and Jesus have you kept secret? What story can you share with others to remind them of His power and tenderness, to give them a touch of faith?

Give me the courage, Jesus, to not just come to You with all my issues but to share my story with others, to touch them with my faith in You and Your faithfulness to me. Amen.

Standards of Success

"Worship and serve him with your whole heart and a willing mind. For the LORD sees every heart and knows every plan and thought. If you seek him, you will find him."
1 CHRONICLES 28:9 NLT

God's view of success is vastly different than the world's. God asks that we give ourselves to Him in worship. We find our success in earnestly seeking after God and following His commands.

On the other hand, the world says that we must have a good job, make lots of money, buy the newest toys, and focus on making ourselves happy. The world does not care how we accomplish these things. If we have to be superficial, fine. If we have to tell a lie here or there, no problem. If we have to pretend to be something we are not, who cares?

God cares. God sees our hearts and knows our motives—good or bad. The world's mindset looks to the tangible elements of success. A good car, a nice job, and a big house indicate success, regardless of how we obtained them. On the other hand, God's focus is on our journey. We may not live in the biggest house on the block, and we may not even own a car, but those things are not important to God. Instead, worshipping and serving God with our whole hearts, being genuine and sincere, and willingly seeking God are the aspects of success in God's eyes.

Dear Lord, teach me to seek after You willingly, with sincere motives. Please help me focus on pleasing You rather than seeking success by worldly standards. Amen.

Feeling Pressed?

By his divine power, God has given us
everything we need for living a godly life.
2 PETER 1:3 NLT

People need you—your family, your friends. Adding their needs to your commitments at school or work can sometimes be too much. Maybe your boss demands extra hours on a project, or your sister needs you to help her with a family birthday party.

People pulling you here and there can have you going in circles. Somehow you keep pushing forward, not always sure where the strength comes from, but thankful in the end that you made it through the day.

In those situations you're not just stretching your physical body to the limit but your mind and emotions as well. Stress can make you feel like a grape in a winepress. But there is good news. God has given you everything you need, but you must choose to use the wisdom He has provided. Don't be afraid to say no when you feel you just can't add one more thing to your to-do list. Limit your commitments, ask someone to take notes for you in a meeting you can't make, or carpool with someone who shares your child's extracurricular activity.

Alleviate the pressure where you can and then know that His power will make up for the rest.

Lord, help me to do what I can do; and I'll trust
You to do for me those things that I can't do. Amen.

Hard Times

He comes alongside us when we go through hard times,
and before you know it, he brings us alongside someone
else who is going through hard times so that we can be
there for that person just as God was there for us.
2 Corinthians 1:4 msg

Hard times are bound to come. Don't let that discourage you. God says that in this world we will have trouble but to take heart because He has overcome the world (John 16:33)!

If you are in the middle of something rough right now, remember that God is always there to comfort you. You may feel that you are at the end of your ability to cope, but that is where God likes to meet us. He is close to the brokenhearted. If you have just experienced something difficult, reflect on what God wants to teach you from that.

Try journaling the things that God has taught you so that you can remember all that He has done for and through you. You can share these memories with someone later on. Don't forget that God uses all our trials for good, to make us more like Christ and to help those around us in their time of need.

Lord, You are the God of comfort. Please help me lean on You during hard times, and help me be a blessing to someone else. Amen.

Godly Conversation

Let no one look down on your youthfulness,
but rather in speech, conduct, love, faith, and purity,
show yourself an example of those who believe.
1 TIMOTHY 4:12 NASB

God hears the conversations of His children—no matter how young or old. As we spend time together and speak with one another, our Father cares about our conversations and wants them to bless and enrich the lives of those who participate.

Conversations peppered with faith and purity, as directed in 1 Timothy 4, are in stark contrast to the ungodly chatter of the world today. The world is darkened by complaints against God, cynicism, unbelief, and gossip—none of which honor God. His heart aches when we use words to tear others down rather than speak truth that encourages.

He wants us to build one another up with the words we use. True Christ-centered fellowship happens when everyone involved is encouraged and strengthened in their faith. And we must always remember that unbelievers watch and listen, always looking to find Christ in the lives of those of us who profess His name. Let's share God's faithfulness, goodness, and love, because our conversations have an impact in the lives of everyone we reach.

Jesus, please touch my lips and allow nothing dishonorable
to pass through them. Guide me and give me grace and
discernment in my conversations so that they would always
be pleasing to You and give glory to Your name. Amen.

Abiding Peace

He himself is our peace.
EPHESIANS 2:14 NIV

Powerful forces converge as a hurricane develops. Even though turbulent winds swirl uncontrollably, the calm eye, the center of the storm, remains unaffected by its surroundings. Regardless of the hurricane's magnitude, the eye always remains calm.

Have you ever experienced a hurricane—perhaps not a real one, but life circumstances that turned your world upside down? The winds of hardship were fiercely blowing. Your suffering felt like pelting rain. Experiencing havoc all around, you didn't know where to turn. Is peace possible in the midst of such turbulence?

Regardless of life's circumstances, hope and peace are available if Jesus is there. You do not have to succumb to getting buffeted and beaten by the storms of life. Seek refuge in the center of the storm. Run to the arms of Jesus, the Prince of Peace. Let Him wipe your tears and calm your fears. Like the eye of the hurricane, His presence brings peace and calmness. Move yourself closer. Desire to be in His presence. For He Himself is your peace. As you abide in His presence, peace will envelop you. The raging around you may not subside, but the churning of your heart will. You will find rest for your soul.

Dear Lord, thank You for being our peace
in the midst of life's fiercest storms. Amen.

Confidence

*For I know that my redeemer liveth, and that he shall stand
at the latter day upon the earth: and though after my skin
worms destroy this body, yet in my flesh shall I see God.*
Job 19:25–26 KJV

What amazing hope we have! We serve a risen Savior.

It is hard to imagine how Job must have felt as he went through such a horrible situation—losing his family, his possessions, and even his health. Yet in all of his misery he said with confidence, "I *know* that my redeemer liveth" (emphasis added). The irony of this is that Christ had not yet been born, much less had He completed His redemptive work. Still, Job's faith did not waver. He knew that one day he would stand before his redeemer in a perfected body.

Although we experience various difficulties throughout life, we can still look forward to the blessed future we have. No matter what our struggles are, our Lord controls.

Job had no idea what the purpose of his trial was, but he faced his troubles with confidence, knowing that ultimately he would emerge victorious. Too many times we view our own situations with self-pity rather than considering God's strength and trusting that His plan is perfect. What peace God offers when we finally cast our cares on Him and with great conviction declare, "I know that my redeemer liveth."

*O great Redeemer, in You I have confidence even when I don't
understand life's trials. Please help me to live victoriously.*

Word to the Wise

If any of you lacks wisdom, he should ask God,
who gives generously to all without finding
fault, and it will be given to him.
JAMES 1:5 NIV

Wisdom should be our request as we seek God's face each day. We all need wisdom for the huge decisions: choosing a husband, picking the right college, which career path to take, or what ministries to pursue. But we also need wisdom for the smaller, day-to-day things as well: what to do in our spare time, how to spend this week's paycheck, or what relationships need attention.

God's Word tells us that He gives wisdom to all who ask—without finding fault. Ask and it will be given to you! However, the verse goes on to say that when you do ask the Lord for wisdom, trust that He will make good on His promise. If you find yourself asking for wisdom but doubting that God will really give it to you, confess that to the Lord and ask Him to change your mindset. Trust in the Lord and know that He is faithful to hear your prayers and answer according to His will.

Father, forgive me for the times I have doubted You. I ask
for wisdom for the big decisions in my life but also for
daily wisdom. Help me to trust You more. Amen.

The True Love

"Love one another; just as I have loved you."
JOHN 13:34 NASB

In a society that has distorted the concept of love, it's reassuring to know that God loves us with a deep, limitless love. He is, in fact, love itself. He gave His Son to die for people who didn't love Him in return. God the Father even had to turn His face from His Son when He died, as He took the sin of humankind upon Himself. What incredible love that is!

We Christians tell Jesus we love Him, and His response is, "I love you more." We cannot comprehend that kind of love, yet we are the recipients of it. And He loves us not because of anything we've done but because of His goodness. First John 4:19 (KJV) says, "We love him, because he first loved us."

Jesus also commands us to love others in the same way that He loves us. We all have unlovable people in our lives. But Jesus doesn't see anyone as unlovable. Look at that difficult-to-love person through new eyes today and love her as God has loved you.

Heavenly Father, thank You for Your love for me.
Forgive me for not loving others in that same way. Give me
the ability to love others as You have instructed. Amen.

The Courage to
See God at Work

So the king of Jericho sent this message to Rahab:
"Bring out the men who came to you and entered your
house, because they have come to spy out the whole land."
JOSHUA 2:3 NIV

God had rescued the Israelites from Egypt by dividing the Red Sea. He led the way through the desert as a pillar of cloud by day and a pillar of fire by night. He provided food and water. For forty years, their clothes did not wear out.

The king of Jericho had heard of this big God and His people, who were camped outside his city ready to attack. Rahab, a prostitute, had heard of this God. But her decision was different from the king's. She looked at the same evidence as the king and made a different decision.

She heard that God was a punishing God and a rescuing God. Jericho had been a wicked city and was going to be punished. She hid the spies that came in to scout out the city. She told them she believed in their God and wanted to be rescued, along with her family. Her actions flowed from her realization of who God is. Her faith not only gets her mentioned in James and Hebrews, but she also becomes part of the lineage of Christ.

What does your knowledge of who God is lead you to do? How can you step out in faith?

Dear God, thank You for rescuing us. Reveal Your character to us in
a new way, and show us how to act because of who You are. Amen.

Pass It On!

*After the usual readings from the books of Moses
and the prophets, those in charge of the service sent
them this message: "Brothers, if you have any word of
encouragement for the people, come and give it."*
ACTS 13:15 NLT

Who doesn't need encouragement? After the reading in the temple, the rulers asked Paul and his companions if they had a word of encouragement to share. Paul immediately stood up and proclaimed how the fulfillment of God's promise came through Jesus; and whoever believed—whether Jew or Gentile—would receive forgiveness and salvation (Acts 13:16–41).

The scriptures state that as Paul and Barnabas left the synagogue, the people invited them to speak again the following Sabbath. And as a result of Paul's testimony, many devout Jews came to Christ. Not only that, but on the next Sabbath, nearly the entire town—Jews and Gentiles alike—gathered to hear God's Word (Acts 13:42–44).

Encouragement brings hope. Have you ever received a word from someone that instantly lifted your spirit? Did you receive a bit of good news or something that diminished your negative outlook? Perhaps a particular conversation helped to bring your problems into perspective. Paul passed on encouragement and many benefited. So the next time you're encouraged, pass it on! You may never know how your words or actions benefited someone else.

*Lord, thank You for the wellspring of
encouragement through Your Holy Word. Amen.*

Women of Faith

I call to remembrance the genuine faith that is in you,
which dwelt first in your grandmother Lois and your
mother Eunice, and I am persuaded is in you also.
2 TIMOTHY 1:5 NKJV

When the apostle Paul thought of young Timothy, one thing stood out. Timothy had true faith. He had been raised by his mother and grandmother to love and trust the Lord. Perhaps you come from a long line of Christian women, or maybe you are a first generation Christ-follower. Either way, these verses have a message for you. We all influence children. Perhaps you have your own children or nieces and nephews. Maybe you spend time with friends' children. Some of you may be grandmothers. Others may work with children either in your career or in a church ministry role. Whatever the situation, you have a great impact on children that look up to you.

It is important to note the trait that stood out was not perfection. It was faith. We cannot be perfect examples for our children. But we can teach them about faith! The way you respond to life's trials speaks the loudest. Children learn about faith when they see it lived out before them. Like Eunice and Lois were wonderful examples for Timothy, may you influence the next generation to place their faith in Christ Jesus.

God, help me to be a woman of faith, for I know that little ones
are watching and learning about You through me. Amen.

Loving Sisters

But Ruth replied, "Don't urge me to leave you or to turn back from you. Where you go I will go, and where you stay I will stay. Your people will be my people and your God my God."
RUTH 1:16 NIV

The story of Ruth and Naomi is inspiring on many levels. It talks of two women from different backgrounds, generations, ethnicity, and even religion. But rather than being obstacles to a loving friendship, these differences became invisible. Both women realized that their commitment, friendship, and love for each other surpassed any of their differences. They were a blessing to each other.

Do you have girlfriends who would do almost anything for you? A true friendship is a gift from God. Those relationships provide us with love, companionship, encouragement, loyalty, honesty, understanding, and more! Lasting friendships are essential to living a balanced life.

Father God, thank You for giving us the gift of friendship. May I be the blessing to my girlfriends that they are to me. Please help me to always encourage and love them and to be a loving support for them in both their trials and their happiness. I praise You for my loving sisters! Amen.

For Such a Time as This

*"If you keep quiet at a time like this, deliverance and
relief for the Jews will arise from some other place,
but you and your relatives will die. Who knows if perhaps
you were made queen for just such a time as this?"*
ESTHER 4:14 NLT

Esther was between the proverbial rock and a hard place. If she approached the king without being invited, she risked losing her life. If she kept silent, she and her family would die. Her wise cousin Mordecai helped put the situation into perspective. He explained that God's plans and purposes would prevail—whether Esther cooperated or not. Esther merely had to choose whether she wanted to experience the joy of participating in God's plan of deliverance for the Jewish people.

Can you imagine the honor of being chosen to help God in this way? God has placed each of us on this earth for a purpose. When we cooperate with Him, we get to experience the blessing of being a part of His plans. If we choose not to participate, there will be consequences. Don't be mistaken—God's purposes will still unfold. But we won't get to be a part of it. Like Esther, the choice is ours. Will we cooperate with God or keep silent and miss out on our place in history?

*Heavenly Father, thank You for placing me on earth at this
time in history. Thank You for the opportunity to be a part
of Your plan. Help me to choose to cooperate with You.*

No Condemnation

*Therefore there is now no condemnation at
all for those who are in Christ Jesus.*
ROMANS 8:1 NASB

There is no condemnation for you who are in Christ Jesus. This means there is no room for guilt or blame in your life. Even when you do things that make you feel like you have failed God, yourself, or others, your standing before God does not change. When you are in Christ, you are clothed in the clean, holy robes of God's Son. When God looks at you, He doesn't see the sins you've committed or the things you haven't done; He sees His holy, blameless Son.

How is this possible? It's possible because Christ died in your place. The sins that would have condemned you in God's holy court were placed on Christ's shoulders and buried with Him. They have no hold over you anymore. So let go of your guilt and regret. Acknowledge that Christ's work on the cross was enough to cleanse and purify you before a holy God. And live in the freedom of the knowledge that no one and nothing can condemn you. Christ has stood in your place so that you can come boldly before the Father in the clean robes that have been washed in the blood of the Lamb. Ask for His forgiveness and claim His forgiveness in your life.

---

*Lord, thank You that I am not and cannot be condemned because I am
in Christ. Help me to more fully understand what Christ did for me
on the cross so that I can let go of the guilt and blame I so often carry.*

A True Heart

Jesus answered, "Isaiah was right when he spoke about you hypocrites. He wrote, 'These people show honor to me with words, but their hearts are far from me. Their worship of me is worthless. The things they teach are nothing but human rules.'"
MARK 7:6–7 NCV

Jesus considered the Pharisees hypocrites because they were pretending to honor the Lord so that others would think they were holy and hold them in high regard. But their hearts weren't in it.

God wants our hearts *and* our words. The Bible says in Luke 6:45 (AMP) that "his mouth speaks from the overflow of his heart." What you think and feel inside is eventually what will come out. If your heart isn't really set on the Lord, people will see that your actions don't match up with what you're saying.

When you pray, always be honest with God and with yourself. When asked to pray in public, there is no need to use large, flowery words to impress others. God is the only one who matters.

A man was asked to pray a blessing before a big holiday dinner. He complied but spoke so softly that not many could hear him at all. When he said "amen," the family looked up to see if he was really finished.

"We couldn't hear you!" the family said.

"Well, I wasn't praying to you!" replied the man.

Dear Jesus, let my heart, my words, and my actions always be true to You. Amen.

Clap Your Hands!

Clap your hands, all you nations; shout to God with cries of joy. How awesome is the LORD Most High, the great King over all the earth! . . . God has ascended amid shouts of joy, the LORD amid the sounding of trumpets. Sing praises to God, sing praises; sing praises to our King, sing praises.

PSALM 47:1–2, 5–6 NIV

In 1931, German theologian Dietrich Bonhoeffer spent a year at a seminary in New York City. While there, he was introduced to a church in Harlem. Astounded, then delighted, at the emotion expressed in worship, he returned to Germany with recordings of gospel music tucked in his suitcase. Bonhoeffer knew that the worship he observed was authentic and pleasing to God.

King David would have loved gospel music! Many of the psalms were meant to be sung loudly and joyfully. David appointed four thousand professional musicians—playing cymbals, trumpets, rams' horns, tambourines, harps, and lyres—for temple worship. We can imagine they would have rocked the roofs off our modern-day church services!

Dancing was a part of worship in David's day too. David angered his wife Michal with his spontaneous dance in the street, as the ark of the covenant was returned to Jerusalem (1 Chronicles 15:29). The world, in David's viewpoint, couldn't contain the delight that God inspires. Neither could he!

How often do we worship God with our whole heart? Has God ever seen you burst forth in a song of praise? Has He witnessed you clapping your hands and lifting them up high? Let's try that today!

O Lord, great is Your name and worthy of praise!

73

Hurt by Others' Choices

God heard the boy crying. The angel of God called from
Heaven to Hagar, "What's wrong, Hagar? Don't be afraid.
God has heard the boy and knows the fix he's in."
GENESIS 21:17 MSG

A slave during early biblical times, Hagar had little say in her life decisions—others made them for her. Because of the infertility of her mistress, Sarah, Hagar became the concubine of Sarah's husband, Abraham, and gave birth to Ishmael.

At first, Hagar's hopes soared. Her son would become Abraham's heir, rich and powerful beyond her wildest dreams! However, the surprise appearance of Isaac, the late-life son of Sarah and Abraham, destroyed Hagar's fantasies of a wonderful future. Sarah wanted Hagar and Ishmael out of their lives. Abraham, though upset, loaded Hagar with water and food and told her to take Ishmael into the unforgiving desert.

When their water supply failed, Hagar laid her dehydrated son under a bush and walked away crying because she could not bear to watch Ishmael die. But God showed Hagar a well of water. Quickly she gave her child a drink. Both survived, and "God was on the boy's side as he grew up" (Genesis 21:20 MSG).

God is also on our side when we and our loved ones suffer because of others' choices. Even when we have lost hope, God's plan provides a way for us and those we love.

Heavenly Father, when my world seems out of control,
please help me love and trust You—even in the deserts of life.

Belly Laughs

*All the days of the afflicted are evil, but he
who is of a merry heart has a continual feast.*
PROVERBS 15:15 NKJV

Do you know how to relax? Have you built a time for laughter into your schedule?

Maybe that sounds silly and unimportant with the demands of life caving in on you. But it's not! In fact, relaxation and fun are vital to your health—and, by extension, the health of your family. We may face challenges, but as Proverbs reminds us, we can have a continual feast regardless of circumstances. Don't wait for laughter to find you—seek it out!

Find a comedy show to loosen up. Maybe get into a tickling match with the kids. Perhaps it's as simple as scheduling a popcorn and movie night with friends (or yourself!) to melt away the day's pressure.

A good laugh is health to our bones and gives our kids permission to lighten up too. Do it now—not when life is in perfect order. Others need to see us loosen up and enjoy ourselves now and then.

*Heavenly Father, You are a God of laughter and enjoyment.
Why does it seem frivolous to giggle with my children? Enable
me to have a continual feast regardless of my circumstances.*

A Pattern Worth Repeating

So know that the LORD your God is God, the faithful God.
He will keep his agreement of love for a thousand lifetimes
for people who love him and obey his commands.
DEUTERONOMY 7:9 NCV

We all know that patterns repeat in families, even to the "third and fourth generation" (Exodus 20:5 NIV). We worry over negative patterns, like abuse and divorce, that have hurt our children the same way they hurt us. We long to replace those negative patterns with godly, joyful living.

God wants that for our families as well. He encourages parents with a God-sized promise, the kind every mother wants for her family but thinks is impossible.

Think beyond a legacy for our grandchildren and great-grandchildren. God's vision extends far past that. He will show "love for *a thousand lifetimes*" (emphasis added). The idea of a "thousand lifetimes" boggles the mind. Taken literally, at twenty-five years times one thousand, it endures for twenty-five thousand years—longer than people have lived on the earth.

God takes our hands and says, "Love Me. Obey Me. I will show love to your family as long as you have descendants on the earth." And when we demonstrate our love for God by doing what He says, we guarantee His faithfulness and love to generations yet unborn, until the Lord returns to take us home.

That's a legacy worth passing on.

Heavenly Father, I praise You that You will be faithful
to my children and their children after them. I pray
that they also will love You and obey You.

Perfect Prayers

In this manner, therefore, pray:
Our Father in heaven.
MATTHEW 6:9 NKJV

How many messages have you heard on prayer? Have you ever come away thinking, *Did you hear how eloquently they prayed? How spiritual they sounded? No wonder God answers their prayers!*

Sometimes we take the straightforward and uncomplicated idea of prayer—the simple give and take of talking with God—and turn it into something hard. How many times have we made it a mere religious exercise, performed best by the "holy elite," rather than what it really is—conversation with God our Father.

Just pour out your heart to God. Share how your day went. Tell Him your dreams. Ask Him to search you and reveal areas of compromise. Thank Him for your lunch. Plead for your kids' well-being. Complain about your car. . . . Just talk with Him. Don't worry how impressive (or unimpressive!) you sound.

Talk with God while doing dishes, driving the car, folding laundry, eating lunch, or kneeling by your bed. Whenever, wherever, whatever— tell Him. He cares!

Don't allow this day to slip away without talking to your Father. No perfection required.

Father God, what a privilege it is to unburden my
heart to You. Teach me the beauty and simplicity
of simply sharing my day with You.

Ladies in Waiting

*I will wait for the L*ORD*. . . . I will put my trust in him.*
ISAIAH 8:17 NIV

Modern humans aren't good at waiting. In our fast-paced society, if you can't keep up, you'd better get out of the way. We have fast food, speed dialing, and jam-packed schedules that are impossible to keep. Instant gratification is the name of the game—and that attitude often affects our own families.

The Lord Jesus Christ doesn't care about instant gratification. Our right-now attitudes don't move Him. Maybe He finds the saying "Give me patience, Lord, *right now*" humorous—but He rarely answers that particular prayer.

Do we want joy without accepting heartache? Peace without living through the stress? Patience without facing demands? God sees things differently. He's giving us the opportunity to learn through these delays, irritations, and struggles. What a wise God He is!

We need to learn the art of waiting on God. He will come through every time—but in *His* time, not ours. The wait may be hours or days, or it could be years. But God is always faithful to provide for us. It is when we learn to wait on Him that we will find joy, peace, and patience through the struggle.

Father, You know what I need, so I will wait.
Help me be patient, knowing that You control my
situation and that all good things come in Your time.

Christ, My Identity

"The LORD your God is with you, he is mighty to save.
He will take great delight in you, he will quiet you with
his love, he will rejoice over you with singing."
ZEPHANIAH 3:17 NIV

As women, we love to love. We tend to trust easily. If we are married, we expect our husbands to look after our children and us, to admire and desire us as wives, always to be our protectors. Even if we've never been married, most of us have dreamed of such relationships.

But when our expectations fall short—whatever the reason—our spirits shatter into a million little pieces. Often, we lose our identity. Any self-esteem we may once have had evaporates along with our dreams.

But God Himself, the Maker of all creation, the very one who hung the stars in space and calls them by name, looks at each one of us with love. In His eyes are delight and joy. Because the Father has created us in His own image, He knows every hurt we feel—and He will quiet us with His love. He rejoices that we are His daughters, and He delights in us—not because of anything we do but simply because we are His.

Lord Jesus, though I sometimes feel alone and without an identity,
I trust that You are with me. I ask that You will quiet my spirit with
Your mighty peace and allow me to know the depth of Your love for me.

Daily Choice

"The thief comes only to steal and kill and destroy;
I have come that they may have life, and have it to the full."
JOHN 10:10 NIV

Some days it seems the negative outweighs the positive. People demand so much of our time. Bills demand so much of our money. Feelings of inadequacy surface quickly. It all caves in around us—it's just too much! But when God's words fall on our hearts, those thoughts of defeat are shown for what they really are: lies that delight the enemy who wants to destroy our souls.

But Christ comes to give life! Choosing life is an act of the will blended with faith. We must daily make the decision to take hold of the life Christ offers us. It's this Spirit-infused life that keeps us going; our greatest efforts often come up short. Accepting this gift from Jesus doesn't guarantee a perfect life; it doesn't even guarantee an easy life. But Christ does promise to sustain us, support us, and provide a haven from the storms of life in His loving arms.

Giving Lord, help me daily choose You and the life You
want to give me. Give me eyes of faith to trust that
You will enable me to serve lovingly, as You do.

Contentment

The LORD is my shepherd, I shall not be in want.
PSALM 23:1 NIV

Probably the most familiar passage in the Bible, the twenty-third Psalm is a picture of contentment. If the Lord is our shepherd, then we are His sheep. Sheep are fragile animals, easily lost and injured, and in need of constant care. They are vulnerable to predators, especially if separated from the flock, and need to be guarded and led to places of safety.

A shepherd spends all his time with his sheep. Theirs is a close relationship, and he is always guarding them. He is responsible for nourishment, rest, places of safety, and care for the injured. The sheep do not have to seek these things; it is the shepherd's job to know what they need and provide it.

Though it's not very flattering to be thought of as sheep, it does help to describe our relationship with God. Because we are sheep, with Christ as our shepherd, we do not have to worry, strive, want, or lack. We are never alone. As Philippians 4:19 (NKJV) says, "My God shall supply all your need according to His riches in glory by Christ Jesus."

*Lord, cause me to remember that I am a sheep
and You are my shepherd. In times of loneliness,
anxiety, need, or pain, help me turn to You.*

Patience Is a Virtue

And not only so, but we glory in tribulations also:
knowing that tribulation worketh patience;
and patience, experience; and experience, hope.
Romans 5:3–4 KJV

"Teach me patience, Lord." There are very few more dangerous words a Christian can utter. Patience can only be taught through tribulation.

In your life, what is God using to teach you patience? A crying baby? Endless diapers? Sleepless nights? Calls from the school principal? Spilled milk? Nonstop questions? You fill in the blank.

Trials produce experiences from which we can learn. The growth that comes through trials teaches us that every unsavory moment in life will eventually pass—and that, through Christ, there is victory in the endurance. That wisdom is true hope.

Can you find hope in the midst of your tribulations today? Let the Holy Spirit help you navigate your day with the wisdom to see that "this too will pass." And when it does, patience, maturity, and, most of all, hope, will be the reward.

Lord Jesus, help me to be like the apostle Paul,
welcoming the tribulations in my life as a means
of becoming the person You've called me to be. Let me
learn from my experiences and grow to be more like You.

This House Is Too Crowded

"Agreed," she replied. "Let it be as you say."
JOSHUA 2:21 NIV

Rahab and her family were crowded inside her tiny house situated on the walls of Jericho. They were waiting for those two Israeli spies to return with their army.

The spies had promised Rahab they would keep her safe from the coming siege. That's all she had to rely on—the word of spies. But Rahab had come to believe that the Israelites' God was the true God. She was willing to stake her life on that belief.

Still, she faced an indeterminate wait—probably with irritable family members who doubted her story. On the day the spies had departed, Rahab had tied that scarlet cord outside her window, to tip them off to her house. Had the cord grown faded, like the patience of her family?

Where were the Israelites? What was taking them so long? Rahab could have no idea what was happening in the camp of the Israelites where, in obedience to God, Joshua had ordered all the men to be circumcised, in a day without anesthetics. Huge numbers of men, each one requiring time to heal!

Rahab didn't know any of that, but she still remained steadfast. Ultimately, she did see God act—saving her and her family.

There are times when all we have to rely on is the Word of God. When that happens, remember Rahab's steadfastness! We can have confidence that His promises will come true: let it be as He says.

Lord, may my faith in Your Word benefit my family as Rahab's faith in the spies' word helped hers. Help me to remain steadfast regarding Your promises.

From Bitterness to Freedom

Why do you say, "The LORD does not see what happens
to me; he does not care if I am treated fairly"?
Isaiah 40:27 ncv

Bitterness. . .even the sound of that word, when spoken aloud, conveys unpleasantness. And we as single mothers are particularly prone to this toxic form of resentment.

Though it's not always the case, the circumstances that brought us to our single parent status often create a deep root of bitterness in us. Perhaps we faced betrayal, deception, or broken promises. Financial struggles, the emotional sorrow of loneliness, losing hope over what might have been—so many things can lead to bitterness in our lives.

We know bitterness is wrong, and our friends tell us to let go. But it's not always that easy. Especially because, well. . .it can feel good to be the injured party. For many people, there's a strange satisfaction in being the "victim."

Bitterness, whether conscious or unconscious, is clearly not a biblical feeling. It eats at us emotionally, spiritually, and even physically. So what should we do?

Tell God how badly you hurt—then ask Him for the capacity to forgive. Allow God to be your vindicator. Place all of your mistreatment into His hands, because He cares. And He'll work things out in the end.

Father, I admit I've been bitter at times as a single parent.
Enable me to forgive when I need to. I know that will set me free.

The Gift of Receiving

"In everything I did, I showed you that by this kind of hard work we must help the weak, remembering the words the Lord Jesus himself said: 'It is more blessed to give than to receive.'"

ACTS 20:35 NIV

You probably already know that, like Jesus said, it is better to give to others than to receive for yourself. But what if everyone gave and no one received? That would be impossible, actually. In order for some to give, others have to receive. God designed it perfectly so that the body of Christ would work together and help one another.

Have you ever turned down help of any kind—tangible goods like money or groceries, or intangible things like babysitting or wise counsel—out of pride? Are you trying to keep a stiff upper lip to show the world how strong you are? Maybe you are fully capable of succeeding with no outside help. But in doing so, you might rob others of the joy of giving.

Next time someone offers help, consider graciously accepting the extended hand. By your willingness to receive, others might enjoy the blessings of giving.

Lord, thank You for the times that You have sent help my way. Please give me the wisdom and the grace to know when to accept help from others—and even the courage to ask for it when I need it.

Forgiven and Free

*Blessed is he whose transgressions
are forgiven, whose sins are covered.*
PSALM 32:1 NIV

Have you ever really pondered *freedom*? Every individual has a slightly different view of the concept. As women, we are free to vote and drive and earn a living. In western countries, we are free to walk down the street without hiding our faces; we are even free to abort babies and demand divorces. With many of our freedoms, however, come painful consequences.

God's Word shows that the freedom He offers is more far-reaching and eternally beneficial than our personal earthly freedoms we so often demand. When we find ourselves alone with children to feed, clothe, and love—and our children need so much more than we can give—God says we are free. When all we seem to receive from outsiders are glares and judgment, God says we are free. Whatever circumstances led us to this point in life—whether choices of our own or the choices of others—transgressions can be forgiven and we can find freedom. Freedom from judgment, guilt, past mistakes, and burdens.

Under God's umbrella, we are free to be who He created us to be. Nothing more, nothing less.

*Father God, thank You for the freedom that comes from
knowing You. You have forgiven my past, and even though I
may live with consequences of that past, You say I am blessed.
Thank You for the blessing of freedom that You give.*

Waiting

Blessed are all who wait for him!
ISAIAH 30:18 NIV

Some studies indicate we spend a total of *three years* of our lives just waiting!

Consider a typical day, with a few minutes stopped at traffic signals, a half hour in the doctor's waiting room, more time yet in a bottlenecked checkout line at the grocery store.

Some of us can handle that waiting through a natural patience. Others? Forget it.

Yet waiting is an inevitable part of everyone's life. And it's a necessary part too. We wait nine months for a baby's birth. We wait for wounds to heal. We wait for our children to mature. And we wait for God to fulfill His promises.

Waiting for God to act is a familiar theme in scripture. Abraham and Sarah waited for a baby until a birth became humanly impossible. But it wasn't impossible to God. Joseph languished, unjustly accused, in Pharaoh's prison, while God ordained a far-reaching drought that would force Joseph's family to Egypt for survival. David spent years hiding from King Saul, but he matured into a wise and capable warrior during that time.

As frustrating as waiting can be, God is always at work on our behalf. Waiting time isn't wasted time. Whatever we might be waiting for—the salvation of our kids, provision for a physical need, a godly husband to help us with our parenting—we can wait with expectancy, trusting in God's timing.

By Your grace, Lord, help me to do the work You've called me to do and to wait patiently for the good results You promise.

More Than Enough

Let us not become weary in doing good, for at the proper
time we will reap a harvest if we do not give up.
GALATIANS 6:9 NIV

How often do we become impatient and give up? We stand in line at the coffee shop and find ourselves behind an indecisive person. Frustrated, we give up—but before we get to our car, that person—coffee cup in hand—walks past. If we'd only waited another minute, we too could be sipping a steaming caramel latte.

Or maybe we have a dream that we can't seem to make a reality—and rather than trying "just one more time," we give up. A piece of who we are drifts away like a leaf on the sea.

The Word of God encourages us to keep going, to press on, to fight off weariness and never give up. Jesus Christ has a harvest for each of us, and He eagerly anticipates blessing us with it—but we have to trust Him and refuse to give in to weariness.

We can only imagine what that harvest might be because we know that God is the God of "immeasurably more than all we ask or imagine" (Ephesians 3:20 NIV). We can be recipients of His "immeasurably more" if we press on in the strength He provides.

When you're tired, keep going—and remember that, in His perfect timing, you will reap an unimaginable harvest.

Father, You know that I'm tired and weary in this
uphill struggle. Fill me with Your strength so I can
carry on. I long to reap the harvest You have for me.

Fill 'er Up—with Joy

We also pray that you will be strengthened with all his
glorious power so you will have all the endurance and
patience you need. May you be filled with joy.
Colossians 1:11 nlt

We've all had days when we feel exhausted on every level, when we've drained our emotional gas tanks bone dry. As Paul prayed for the Christians of Colosse, we need a filling of God's strength so we can keep going—and rediscover *joy*.

But when can we find time to refill our tank in a life of constant work and worry? We don't have enough time for the rat race itself, let alone a pit stop. But if we don't refuel, we'll stall out—and be of no use to anyone.

That means we have to learn to make time for ourselves. We can explore things that give us a lift. Some things, like listening to a favorite song as we drift off to sleep, take no extra time. Others, like a bubble bath, may require minor adjustments to our schedule. Maybe we'll want to spend time in the garden or call a friend. There are any number of ways to recharge our spiritual batteries.

Every week—perhaps every day—we must set aside time to refill our tanks. The joy of the Lord will be our reward.

Lord of joy, we confess that we are tempted to work
until we fall apart. We pray that You will show us
the things that will give us the strength to go on.

Tucking an Octopus into Bed

"Do not worry about your life, what you will eat or drink;
or about your body, what you will wear. . . . Who of you by
worrying can add a single hour to his life? . . . God clothes the grass
of the field. . .will he not much more clothe you, O you of little faith?"
MATTHEW 6:25, 27, 30 NIV

Who among us doesn't struggle with anxiety?

Compare worry to trying to tuck an octopus into bed. One tentacle or another keeps popping out from under the covers. If we're not worried about one child, it's the other. If we're not worried about our kids, it's our aging parents. Or the orthodontist's bill. Or the funny sound under the hood of the car.

In the Bible, Jesus spoke much about worry. In a nutshell, He told us not to! Jesus never dismissed the untidy realities of daily life—He knew those troubles firsthand, having spent years as a carpenter in Nazareth, probably living hand-to-mouth as He helped to support His family.

But Jesus also knew that, without looking to God in faith, worry would leave us stuck in a wrestling match with the octopus. Only when we look to God to provide for our needs are we released from worry's grip. "Seek first his kingdom and his righteousness, and all these things will be given to you as well," Jesus promised (Matthew 6:33 NIV).

At that point, worry no longer has a hold on us. It is replaced by a liberating confidence in the power of God.

Lord, with Your help we can live our
daily life free from the grasp of worry.

The Gift of Peace

"Peace I leave with you; my peace I give you.
I do not give to you as the world gives. Do not
let your hearts be troubled and do not be afraid."

JOHN 14:27 NIV

Watching the news every day is enough to make anyone uneasy and restless, especially if the news stories are happening nearby. People disappear every day, children are abused, and cities are torn apart by rioting and looting. There seems to be no end to the evil that abounds in every city and town across our country. How can anyone live in peace under those circumstances?

As Christians, we can have peace even in the face of all the tragedy happening around us. Jesus made a promise to His disciples and to us as well. He was going back to the Father, but He was giving us a priceless gift. He gave us His peace. The world can never give us the peace that Jesus gives. It's a peace that we, the recipients, can't even understand. It's too wonderful for our minds to grasp, but we know it comes from Him.

Whatever is happening in your world, Christ can give you peace. None of the problems you're facing are too big for Him, whether it's trouble in the city where you live or pain in your own home. He is saying to you, "Don't let your heart be troubled about these things, and don't be afraid."

Jesus, I ask for Your peace to fill my heart and mind.
Help me not to be afraid of the problems I'm facing.

Dressed to the Nines

*Put on all of God's armor so that you will be able
to stand firm against all strategies of the devil.*
EPHESIANS 6:11 NLT

Have you ever left your house feeling as though you had forgotten something and weren't completely ready to face the world? Maybe you left home without putting on the belt that matches the dress you're wearing or traveled to an out-of-town conference without the proper shoes to wear. It may have been something as simple as forgetting to put on your watch or lipstick. Whatever the case may be, you feel underdressed and incomplete because of the missing item. You feel as if everyone is looking at you, which makes you feel self-conscious and keeps you from being your best on those days.

Paul wrote to the Ephesians, and to us, that it's important to put on the whole armor of God. This is our spiritual wardrobe. He lists the various pieces we should wear every day in order to stand against the devil and his tricks. We cannot afford to forget even one item. Why? Because the missing piece makes us vulnerable in that area. The enemy knows to attack us there. Each day, we must equip ourselves with the armor God has given us, from the breastplate of righteousness to the sword of the Spirit. Before you start your day, be sure you're fully dressed. Don't allow the devil to keep you from feeling confident and being at your best for God.

*Lord, help me to realize the importance of wearing the armor
You have provided and to never leave home without it.*

Answered Prayer

Delight yourself in the LORD; and He
will give you the desires of your heart.
PSALM 37:4 NASB

Sometimes our heartfelt prayers receive a "yes" from God. Sometimes, it's a "no." At other times, we get back only a "not yet."

Have you heard anyone quote today's scripture, saying that God will give us the desires of our hearts? Some believe the verse means that a Christian can ask for anything—health, money, possessions, you name it—and get exactly what she wants. But this passage actually teaches something much deeper.

Note the first part of Psalm 37:4: "Delight yourself in the LORD." A woman who truly delights herself in the Lord will naturally have the desires of her heart—because her heart desires only God and His will. Our Father takes no pleasure in the things of this world—things that will all wither and die. Neither should we.

So what pleases God? He loves it when we witness for Him and live right. If those are things that we also truly desire, won't He grant us the "desires of our heart" and let us see people brought into the kingdom? Won't we have a life rich in spiritual growth?

Lord, please help me see where my desires are not in line
with Your will—so that the things that I pursue are
only and always according to Your own desires.

Swing and Miss

And though she spoke to Joseph day after day,
he refused to go to bed with her or even be with her.
GENESIS 39:10 NIV

Hardships? Joseph knew them.

Sold into slavery by his brothers, he was carried off to a foreign land. By God's grace, Joseph gained an opportunity to manage the household of an Egyptian official named Potiphar. He was still a slave, but he had impressed Potiphar tremendously.

Joseph also impressed Potiphar's wife. She had a lusty eye for the "well-built and handsome" young man (Genesis 39:6 NIV), and she was determined to seduce him.

Was God tempting Joseph? Had the Lord set Joseph up to test his mettle? Maybe God was giving Joseph a chance to practice with temptation so he'd be more skilled at saying no when bigger temptations came later. You know—like a baseball player taking batting practice, hitting some balls, but occasionally swinging and missing.

That may seem logical, but scripture tells us God would *never* entice us to sin or fail. Since doing so would be contrary to His nature, He allows situations into our lives only for good. He wants us to succeed, each and every time. He wants us to hit a home run, by faith, every time we come to bat.

Joseph did. He told the woman, "How then could I do such a wicked thing and sin against God?" (Genesis 39:9). Then he ran!

Let's learn from Joseph's example.

Lord, help me to see every circumstance in my life as ordained by
You for my welfare. Teach me to respond in faith, every time.

Faith Eyes

*Now faith is being sure of what we hope
for and certain of what we do not see.*
HEBREWS 11:1 NIV

Think for a moment of things we can't see, but we know are there.

There's the wind, for one. Its effects are obvious, as golden grain sways to and fro or fall leaves blow into the sky. And there's gravity, which pulls our kids' cups—full of red Kool-Aid, usually—right to the floor.

It's the same with faith, as we simply believe in what we do not see. God *says* He is faithful, and so His faithfulness exists. He gives us the signs of His unseen presence, and its effects surround us.

We read how the Israelites walked to the sea and, at Moses' command, the sea parted. They could have been killed—by the pursuing Egyptians or by the sea itself—but God made a safe way of escape for them.

What signs surround you, showing your God is real? Perhaps someone blessed you with money to pay a bill or purchase school supplies. Maybe your "guardian angel" caught your attention and helped you avoid a serious accident. Or perhaps your child prayed to accept the Lord.

Those are all signs of the faithfulness of God. Look around with your "faith eyes" and see the signs surrounding you.

*God, I struggle to have faith. Show me where You have
been faithful so my faith can be strengthened. I know You
are faithful, but today I'm asking for a special sign that
You have not forgotten me. Thank You, Father.*

Living Water

*The woman said to him, "Sir, give me this
water so that I won't get thirsty and have
to keep coming here to draw water."*
JOHN 4:15 NIV

The Samaritan woman who came to draw water from Jacob's well didn't know she would meet someone who would change her life drastically. Her life had been filled with relationships that didn't work. She may have felt worthless and used. That day may have started out like every other day in her life, but when she approached the well, Jesus was waiting. He asked her for a drink. When she questioned His reason, He in turn offered her water—living water. If she drank of it, she would never thirst again. She was all for never having to come to the well again to draw water, not realizing Jesus was offering her spiritual life, not a physical refreshment. As they talked, she found living water that gave her a new lease on life.

Some days our life can seem like one endless task after another; it exhibits a sameness that makes us weary. We thirst for something better or maybe just different. Maybe it's time for a trip to the well. As we come to Christ in prayer, seeking a much-needed drink, we will find Him waiting at the well, offering the same living water to each of us that He offered to the Samaritan woman. Are there any among us who don't need times of spiritual refreshing in our lives? Grab a bucket and go to the well. Jesus is waiting.

*Jesus, help me to drink from Your well of
living water so I will never thirst again.*

Restoring the Broken Pieces

And the vessel that he made of clay was marred in the hand of the potter; so he made it again into another vessel, as it seemed good to the potter to make.

JEREMIAH 18:4 NKJV

Some people enjoy restoring old furniture, giving it new life. They strip away the old finish that is scratched and ugly, sand the wood to a beautiful sheen, and cover it with a coat of new varnish or paint. Sometimes the old, worn fabric is replaced with a new piece of cloth. When it is finished, it is a "new" piece of furniture. But it doesn't happen overnight. It takes patient, loving care to get it just right.

Jeremiah went to the potter's house and saw the potter at work on a vessel of clay. While the potter was working on the piece, it became marred. The potter didn't toss the clay away but kept working, fashioning it into another vessel. God wants to restore lives scratched and marred by sin just as some restore furniture and the potter molds clay into usable vessels. No matter what has stained or disfigured our lives, God can mold us into the person He wants us to be. To become a usable vessel, we must allow the potter to knead and work the clay. Even if we fall off the potter's wheel by our own choice, He can pick us up and remold us into a new creation.

Father, help me to stay on the potter's wheel until You are finished with me.

Praise to Be Raised

My God, I cry out by day, but you do not answer, by night,
but I find no rest. . . . To you they cried out and were
saved; in you they trusted and were not put to shame.
PSALM 22:2, 5 NIV

Life isn't easy. We've heard many platitudes meant to encourage us. Being a complainer is not attractive. You need to find the silver lining in every cloud. If life gives you lemons, make lemonade. Smile even when it hurts.

Most of us try to begin our day by thanking God for our blessings before we face our challenges. But when we feel despair, is it acceptable to complain or do we need to bury those emotions? The Bible recounts times when people cried out to the Lord, times when they voiced their complaints. In Psalm 22 we're told that Christ poured out His soul to His heavenly Father throughout His sufferings. If we follow Christ's example, we can take our complaints to God in prayer as long as we, like Christ, also acknowledge our love for and trust in God.

If we just complain to others, we won't solve our problems. If we praise God and trust Him to stand with us during our trials, He will raise us up to handle our problems. Maybe we need to replace those old platitudes with this one: complain and remain, or praise to be raised.

Lord, thank You for listening to my complaints and
saving me from my sins. Even during my struggles
I will praise You as my God and Savior. Amen.

Love One Another

Greet one another with a kiss of love.
Peace to all of you who are in Christ.
1 PETER 5:14 NIV

Our capacity for love is unlimited. If we ever wonder how much love one person can shower on others, we need only to consider the love between a parent and a child. There is scientific evidence that when a baby is born a hormonal process occurs for both parents that ensures parental love for the new life. If it were truly just a matter of some unseen chemical that causes parents to offer unconditional love for life, how then can we experience that same type of love for an adopted child or a grandchild? How does it happen that we have dear friends we love even though we don't always "like" them?

How? Love is a choice. We choose to give and receive love. As Christians, we must heed God's command to love one another. In 1 Peter we read that we are to greet one another with love.

As when you were a child and shared valentines with your friends, think today of those you love as God loves you. Reach out and show them your love. It can be as simple as a call, text, or email saying, "I love you." Today is a good day to ensure that your loved ones *know* that you love them, unconditionally.

Lord, thank You for all those You have given me to love.
Help me to show Your love as You have commanded. Amen.

Can't You Hear
Him Whisper?

He says, "Be still, and know that I am God."
PSALM 46:10 NIV

Our society is so fast paced there is little time to take care of our mental and physical health, let alone our spiritual health. We are beings created for eternity, and we are made in the image of a supernatural God, and yet paying attention to our spiritual journey gets put off and off and off.

Until something terrible happens. Like a financial crisis. Or infidelity in our marriage. Or bad news at the doctor's office. Or a death in the family. Then we do far more than pause. We go into a full-body panic mode, drenched in fear, racing around, grasping at anything and everything, desperate for answers. For peace.

But had we been in close fellowship with the Lord all along, we wouldn't be so frantic, our spirits so riddled with terror. What we need to do is to be still and know that He is God. Know that He is still in control, even though we think the bad news is in control. It's not. God is.

Life would be more peaceful, more focused, more infused with joy, if we were already in the midst of communion with God when troubles come.

Can't you hear Him whisper to you, "Be still, and know that I am God"?

---

*Lord, help me to want to spend time with You every day
of my life—in fair weather as well as stormy. Amen.*

A Spectacle of Joy

Wearing a linen ephod, David was dancing before the LORD with all his might, while he and all Israel were bringing up the ark of the LORD with shouts and the sound of trumpets. As the ark of the LORD was entering the City of David, Michal daughter of Saul watched from a window. And when she saw King David leaping and dancing before the LORD, she despised him in her heart.

2 SAMUEL 6:14–16 NIV

The world tells us how to live our lives—how to eat, communicate, love, sleep, grieve, and celebrate. But the problem is, the world's philosophies and values and viewpoints don't usually mesh with God's ways. In the book of 2 Samuel when David danced before the Lord, we sense that even though his wife Michal despised her husband's spectacle of utter joy, the Lord did not. David was celebrating with abandon—although not in the conventional ways perhaps—but he was indeed showing his passionate joy and profound thankfulness to God.

How easy it is to seek the approval of others. How tempting. But how unwise. Let us instead seek to satisfy God, to love Him, to joy in His presence. Life will then be more beautiful. Maybe not as the world describes beauty, but it will possess a loveliness in spirit from the Lord that the world cannot touch. That the world will puzzle over. That the world may even ponder and eventually desire.

Dear Lord, help me to seek Your approval and not the world's. Show me how to praise You for Your goodness and mercy. Amen.

One Chapter

"In the future, when your children ask you, 'What do these stones mean?' tell them that the flow of the Jordan was cut off before the ark of the covenant of the LORD. . . . These stones are to be a memorial to the people of Israel forever."
JOSHUA 4:6–7 NIV

Faith boils down to a willingness to trust God without knowing the end of the story.

Centuries ago, Joshua faced that very issue. God told him to march the Israelite soldiers around the city of Jericho in complete silence, once a day for six days. On the seventh day, they were to march around the city seven times. Then the priests were to blow their rams' horns and the soldiers to shout.

That's all the information Joshua had to conquer Jericho. But that's not the only chapter in this story. Joshua had a long history with God's interventions. He had seen God part the Red Sea for the wandering Israelites and had just witnessed another miracle as the Israelites walked through the Jordan River too. Joshua knew, by experience, that God was trustworthy.

When his army did what God had instructed, Joshua saw Jericho's walls come tumblin' down.

It's easy to focus on a single chapter in our story, and to forget God's many provisions. But the Lord wants us to keep the big picture in mind, remembering His answered prayers.

Is it worth starting a journal, like Joshua's stone monument, that will remind you and your kids of God's trustworthiness?

Lord, Your compassion has never failed me or my family. May I remember to praise You and thank You all the days of my life.

How Do I Love Thee?

This is what real love is: It is not our love for God;
it is God's love for us. He sent his Son to die
in our place to take away our sins.

1 JOHN 4:10 NCV

If the word *love* were banned from popular music, radio stations and songwriters would go out of business. Even the internet would shrink without this word so key to human existence. All around the world, people search for someone to care. They chat with strangers, post videos, pay for profiles—anything to find the real love they crave.

Few prove successful—because we human beings are hard to love! Even our charity often wears a disguise. We give so we will receive attention, prestige, or assurance that other people will respect us. Some of us even think our little five-and-dime "love" will obtain a place for us in heaven, as if God were a headwaiter to be bribed.

The Bible tells us He does not *need* our love. He *is* love. God the Father, God the Son, and God the Spirit love each other in perfect eternal unity and joy. If God had done the logical thing, He would have wiped out us troublesome humans and created a new race, one that would worship Him without question.

But He would rather die than do that.

Oh, Lord, when I presume on Your love, please forgive me.
Open my eyes to Your magnificent generosity so I can worship
with my whole heart, in a way that pleases You.

Pliable as Clay

"O house of Israel, can I not do with you as this potter does?" declares the LORD. "Like clay in the hand of the potter, so are you in my hand, O house of Israel."
JEREMIAH 18:6 NIV

God has great plans for your life. He is the expert craftsman. He has drawn the blueprints and created the clay—that is, you. He has a design in mind that specifically uses your talents, gifts, interests, strengths, and experiences. His design for your life takes all of these factors into account to form one master plan for a valuable piece.

But He won't shape you by force. You must surrender your clay to be shaped by the Master. You will need to ask yourself what it means to be "like clay in the hand of the potter." What does it look like?

To surrender yourself, you must give up any selfish claims on fashioning your own design. The clay cannot tell the potter what it intends to be.

Begin by discovering your talents, interests, and strengths. What are the activities you especially enjoy? What skills come naturally to you? Once you discover your unique qualities, turn to observation. Where do you see needs in your home? In your school? At work? At church? In your community? How are you especially gifted to meet those needs?

Open yourself to the possibility of being molded into the best version of yourself. God wants to fashion your character, your heart, your life. Let Him.

Lord, forgive me for selfishly holding back my talents and gifts. Amen.

Breathing Room
for Our Souls

He's solid rock under my feet, breathing room for
my soul, an impregnable castle: I'm set for life.
PSALM 62:2 MSG

In a materialistic, ambitious society like ours, the idea of taking time to rest and play isn't always our highest priority. After all, we're told that to get ahead you have to work longer and harder than everyone else.

But God, in His infinite wisdom and love, formed us with a need for downtime. He who created us longs for us to recreate—to enjoy recreation—regularly. So don't let a fear of falling behind rob you of the joy and necessity of recreation. Our bodies and souls need fun in order to thrive.

Find some way to blow off steam, whether it's gardening, painting, or scrapbooking. What did you like to do as a child? Answering that question can guide you to a hobby that relaxes you and gives you deep, abiding joy. Maybe you would enjoy watching movies, running races, or playing Bunco with your girlfriends.

And as believers, we can—and should—invite God into our recreation times. He wants to be a part of every area of our daily lives, whether we're working, resting, or blowing off steam.

After all, He is the place where our souls find their ultimate rest and peace.

Father, I praise You for the way You made me—with a need to
work, rest, and play. I invite You to join me while I recreate.

Itty-Bitty Words

The words of the reckless pierce like swords,
but the tongue of the wise brings healing.
Proverbs 12:18 niv

Whoever started the childhood chant—"Sticks and stones may break my bones, but words will never hurt me"—lied. Plain and simple.

Words may seem itty-bitty as they escape from our lips, but they have the power to make us cringe and cry and crumble into pieces. Pieces that may never come back together again the way they were meant to be.

Words can destroy a reputation. Break a tender heart. And a not-so-tender heart. Words can create an untold ripple effect of misery. And our words can grieve the Holy Spirit. Surely there is a better way to live. There is. It's with the power of the Holy Spirit. From the Psalms comes a wonderful daily heart-prayer: "May these words of my mouth and this meditation of my heart be pleasing in your sight, Lord, my Rock and my Redeemer" (Psalm 19:14 niv).

Our words can heal, comfort, challenge, encourage, and inspire. It's our choice, every minute of every day, which kind of words we will use. Those that heal or those that hurt. Let us always speak truth, yes, but let us do it with tenderness. Not with a mindset that feeds our egos, but with a caring spirit that pleases God.

Holy Spirit, guide me in my thoughts, and may
my words be healing to all I meet. Amen.

Shout for Joy

*The desert and the parched land will be glad; the wilderness
will rejoice and blossom. Like the crocus, it will burst
into bloom; it will rejoice greatly and shout for joy.*
Isaiah 35:1–2 niv

Is there any season as joyous as spring? The trees unfurl thousands of tiny, juicy green flags to wave hello to the world. Flowers make that final push through the dark soil and stretch out their bedecked heads to embrace the sun-warmed air. Farmers plant seeds of promise into the brown, barren land—measuring out hope by the bushel.

You are human. You will go through times of sorrow and despair, times of suffering and boredom. You will work through long days and toss and turn through longer nights. You will worry and fret and stew. You will look around and see only gray.

But spring is our annual reminder that the story isn't over. It's never over. It starts up from page 1 again every year, ready to be filled with characters and plots and dialogue. No, the story won't always be happy and the characters won't all get along. But isn't it amazing that it happens at all? That our Creator God is willing to keep writing new chapters for us? And that He never runs out of ideas?

A new story every spring starts right before your eyes. Now that's something to shout about.

*Dear Lord, thank You for Your endless creativity that brings
us so much grace and joy. Help me remember in the grayest
times that color is just an inch or so under my feet.*

As Pure as Rainwater

Hatred stirs up conflict, but love covers over all wrongs.
PROVERBS 10:12 NIV

Have you ever seen a rain barrel filled after a good storm? That water is clean and refreshing. But if you take a big stick and whip up the contents, soon the dregs will rise and whirl. Suddenly what was clean is now a dirty mess. That visual is a good one for Proverbs 10:12, which reminds us that hatred stirs up old quarrels.

When we choose to hold on to grudges, then hatred seeps into our hearts. It's like we're carrying around a big stick, and we're more than ready to whip up some dregs by bringing up an argument from the past. This is a common way to live, but not a godly or healthy one.

What's the answer?

Love.

When we love others, we will overlook insults, whether they are intended or not. Does that seem like an impossible task using these feeble shells of ours?

It is impossible in our own humanness.

But with the supernatural power of the Holy Spirit, we can overcome this need to stir up trouble, and we can forgive freely and love abundantly—just as Christ has done for us. So let us come not with a big stick but with a spirit as refreshing and as pure as rainwater.

Holy Spirit, please take away any tendency in me to bicker, and instead make me into a woman who loves with my whole heart and who is an instrument of Your peace. Amen.

Rejoice! Rejoice!

Rejoice in the Lord always.
I will say it again: Rejoice!
PHILIPPIANS 4:4 NIV

Paul must have really wanted the Philippians to know he was serious about this idea of rejoicing. He says it not once but twice. Perhaps Paul wanted to emphasize the double impact of what the Lord has done for them—and us. We have new life because Jesus died on the cross for our sins!

Paul was also aware that our actions as Christians cannot be self-absorbed. We must be constantly focused on our brothers and sisters and on those outside the faith.

Paul's command to rejoice affects others as well as ourselves. Smiles are contagious, and true joy spreads easily. When we rejoice, we encourage others and remind them of our blessings in Christ. Those who do not know the peace of Christ see our great joy and want to know what is different about us. By constantly rejoicing in the Lord, we are able to spread the Word of God and tell others about the love of Christ.

Dear Lord, thank You for Your love. Teach me
to continually rejoice, and may my joy
spread to those around me. Amen.

Answer Me!

Answer me when I call to you, my righteous God. Give me relief from my distress; have mercy on me and hear my prayer.
PSALM 4:1 NIV

Have you ever felt like God wasn't listening? We've all felt that from time to time. David felt it when he slept in a cold, hard cave night after night, while being pursued by Saul's men. He felt it when his son Absalom turned against him. Time and again in his life, David felt abandoned by God. And yet David was called a man after God's own heart.

No matter our maturity level, there will be times when we feel abandoned by God. There will be times when our faith wavers and our fortitude wanes. That's okay. It's normal.

But David didn't give up. He kept crying out to God, kept falling to his knees in worship, kept storming God's presence with his pleas. David knew God wouldn't hide His face for long, for he knew what we might sometimes forget: God is love. He loves us without condition and without limit. And He is never far from those He loves.

No matter how distant God may seem, we need to keep talking to Him. Keep praying. Keep pouring out our hearts. We can know, as David knew, that God will answer in His time.

Dear Father, thank You for always hearing my prayers.
Help me to trust You, even when You seem distant. Amen.

Planning for Tomorrow

*"So don't worry about tomorrow, for tomorrow will bring
its own worries. Today's trouble is enough for today."*
MATTHEW 6:34 NLT

The feeling of being at a crossroads comes to many of us in the years following high school and college and during the initial stages of a career. Hitting the "real world" for the first time, it's easy to lose sight of the present and focus on the future. Setting goals can easily turn into constant concern over what is to come.

Where to move, what career path to take, what job to apply for, and even whether to attend more schooling are just a few of the constant questions that can lead to a daily sense of worry and stress.

But God reminds us that those worries are to be left for tomorrow.

Thinking about the future has its place and setting goals is important, but these things should not become our all-consuming focus in life. Jesus said, "Tomorrow will bring its own worries," so we need to learn to be content with today and remind ourselves that God will take care of our needs. If we trust in Him each day, a path will be made known. And those worries for tomorrow will fade.

*Dear Lord, remind me that You are in control yesterday,
today, and tomorrow. Help me not to worry about the
future but to actively seek You each day. Amen.*

Renewed Strength

But those who hope in the LORD will renew their strength.
They will soar on wings like eagles; they will run and
not grow weary, they will walk and not be faint.
ISAIAH 40:31 NIV

Several times throughout scripture, the Lord had the writers use the eagle as a comparison to His people. Moses, speaking to the children of Israel just before his death, draws a beautiful picture of the eagle caring for her young. He then compares it to the Lord's leading in our lives. "He found him in a desert land and in the wasteland, a howling wilderness; He encircled him, He instructed him, He kept him as the apple of His eye. As an eagle stirs up its nest, hovers over its young, spreading out its wings, taking them up, carrying them on its wings, so the LORD alone led him, and there was no foreign god with him" (Deuteronomy 32:10–12 NKJV).

Isaiah carries that metaphor a bit further in Isaiah 40. Women seem to be most involved in nurturing their children, and as a result we tire easily. Starting in verse 27 in the Isaiah passage, Isaiah wonders how God's people can say that God is too busy or tired to care for His people. Instead he turns it around and says that even young men and children get tired. Only those who hope in the Lord will He carry on His wings, renewing their strength.

Father, thank You for these comparisons that show Your
loving heart in caring for Your children. I praise You for
enabling us to do the work You have called us to do.

Love's Current

The grace of our Lord was poured out on me abundantly,
along with the faith and love that are in Christ Jesus.
1 TIMOTHY 1:14 NIV

Giving a gift to a loved one often gives us great pleasure. We shop in anticipation of the recipient's excitement in our purchases. When we love that person, our joy can be even greater. So it is with God's love for us. He gave us His Son: a pure and perfect gift because He loves us in vast measure.

No matter what our attitude may be toward God, we can never forget His precious gift of Jesus Christ. Even if we reflect despair or anger, He loves us. Scripture states grace and love is given abundantly, which means bountifully, plenteously, generously. How can we miss God's love when He is so gracious?

The famous theologian Charles Spurgeon put it this way: "Our God never ceases to shine upon his children with beams of love. Like a river, his lovingkindness is always flowing, with a fullness inexhaustible as his own nature."

This day, rise with the expectation of God's great grace and love. Let your life reflect that love, and feel His pleasure. Plunge into the river of His love and feel Him carry you on its current. Relax in His arms in the knowledge that He cares for you.

Lord, carry me along in the current of Your
love's stream. I love You extravagantly. Amen.

To Know Him Is to Trust Him

Those who know your name trust in you, for you,
O LORD, do not abandon those who search for you.
PSALM 9:10 NLT

Names often reveal the character of a person. This is true in biblical times, especially when it comes to the names of God. A study of His names often brings a deeper awareness of God and who He is. Isaiah, in predicting the birth of Christ, listed several of His names: "For a child is born to us, a son is given to us. The government will rest on his shoulders. And he will be called: Wonderful Counselor, Mighty God, Everlasting Father, Prince of Peace" (9:6 NLT).

In other places He is referred to as Lord Jehovah, Almighty God, Shepherd, Priest, King of kings, and Lord of lords. He is the God who Sees, the Righteous One, Master, Redeemer, the All-Sufficient One. Each name describes a little different attribute or includes the many sides of His character. All are perfectly true about Him.

A study of the names of God, Jesus, and the Holy Spirit not only gives us a deeper insight into the nuances of who He is but also strengthens our ability to trust Him implicitly with every detail of our lives. He has promised to reveal Himself to those who truly seek Him out, who truly desire to "know Him and the power of His resurrection and the fellowship of His sufferings, being conformed to His death" (Philippians 3:10 NASB).

Father, reveal Yourself to me through
Your names, so I will trust You more.

Get Up and Try Again

*But may the God of all grace, who called us to His
eternal glory by Christ Jesus, after you have suffered a
while, perfect, establish, strengthen, and settle you.*
1 PETER 5:10 NKJV

Have you ever fallen down in your Christian walk? It doesn't mean you
are no longer a Christian, but you stumbled over something in your path
that caused you to lose your footing. Perhaps you didn't see the obstacle
in time. It's painful to fall, and sometimes it's hard to get up and continue on. While you're lying on the ground spiritually, Satan uses this
opportunity to taunt you and accuse you. "You're not really a Christian.
If you were, you wouldn't have fallen. You wouldn't have made a mistake.
God doesn't need people like you. He's tired of fooling with you. Why
don't you just give up?"

Sound familiar? Not only does it sound familiar, but if you're not
careful, you will begin to believe it. The shame and remorse you feel
because of your shortcoming only add to the lie Satan has just whispered
in your ear. Don't listen to any more of his lies. God is a God of grace.
The key is to stand up from the place where you have fallen and allow
God to restore you, strengthen you, and establish you. He is faithful to
His people.

*Lord, forgive my shortcomings and extend grace once more
to Your servant. Give me strength to continue the race.*

Staying Close

"Be strong and courageous. Do not be afraid;
do not be discouraged, for the LORD your
God will be with you wherever you go."
JOSHUA 1:9 NIV

It's easy to tell others not to worry. It's easy to remind our friends that God is with them and He's got everything under control. And it's easy to remind ourselves of that, when everything's going smoothly.

But when life sails us into rough waters, our natural instinct is to be afraid. We worry and fret. We cry out, not knowing how we will pay the bills or how we will face the cancer or how we will deal with whatever stormy waves crash around us. When life is scary, we get scared.

And believe it or not, that's a good thing. Because when we are afraid, when we are overwhelmed, when we realize that our circumstances are bigger than we are, that's when we're in the perfect place for God to pour out His comfort and assurance on us.

He never leaves us, but sometimes when life is good, we get distracted by other things and don't enjoy His presence as we should. When we feel afraid, we are drawn back to our heavenly Father's arms. And right in His arms is exactly where He wants us to be.

Dear Father, thank You for staying with me
and giving me courage. Help me to stay close
to You, in good times and bad. Amen.

God Is in the Details

Nevertheless, each person should live as a believer in whatever
situation the Lord has assigned to them, just as God has
called them. This is the rule I lay down in all the churches.
1 CORINTHIANS 7:17 NIV

Sometimes we wonder why God puts particular information in the Bible—like the parts of the Old Testament with numbers and dates that don't seem relevant to our lives. What purpose does it serve for us? But its presence in God's inspired Word shows God is in the details and He loves us in a personal and intimate way. He has called us to the situations we are in, with the people who are around us, for a particular reason.

Other verses expand on this concept:

- Matthew 10:29–31 tells us God has His eye on us individually. He's focused on our needs. He sees us.

- Matthew 6:28–32 says God is well aware of our financial needs. He knows our specific needs and has plans beyond what we can see.

- Romans 14:2–4 tells us God sees our individual weaknesses and struggles. He provides specific ways to help us grow our faith and provides people and situations to help us stand.

Think about a friend God brought into your life at a particular time when you needed that person, or when God provided for your needs in an unexpected way. Focus on how God loves you individually.

Dear Jesus, thank You for loving us in such a personal
way and for having unique plans for each of us. Amen.

Grace Accepted

But because of his great love for us, God, who is
rich in mercy, made us alive with Christ even
when we were dead in transgressions—
it is by grace you have been saved.
EPHESIANS 2:4–5 NIV

Have you ever been wrongly accused of something or completely misunderstood? Have the words of your accusers struck your heart, making you feel like you have to make it right somehow, but no amount of reasoning with them seems to help?

If anyone understands this situation it's Christ Himself. Wrongly accused. Misunderstood. Yet He offered unfathomable grace at all times and still offers it today.

This reminds us that we are to aim to offer this same grace to our accusers and those who misunderstand us. We will be misunderstood when we try to obey and follow God in a culture that runs quite contrary in many ways. Our job is to first accept God's grace and then offer it up to others as lovingly as we can. Like Christ.

God, help us to continually accept Your grace through Christ
and reflect You by offering that same grace to others. Amen.

Wise Like Jesus

*But the wisdom that comes from heaven is first of
all pure; then peace-loving, considerate, submissive,
full of mercy and good fruit, impartial and sincere.*
JAMES 3:17 NIV

Who has wisdom? Look at the fruit of her life. From this verse, we know a wise woman chooses to pursue peace in her community—she forgives someone who hurt her instead of writing him off. She is considerate; she sees others with God's eyes—worthy of her love because they are loved by their Creator, no matter what they have done or left undone. She submits her hurts to her Father, learning from Him how to show mercy as He does. Sincerity blossoms throughout her words and deeds.

If this description of a wise woman leaves you thinking *That's not me!*, don't worry, you certainly aren't alone. Wisdom is a gift from God, born from a desire to follow His Word out of love for Him. Our own efforts can only conjure up an imperfect wisdom and love for others because our natural state is selfish. Humanity lost its capacity to love purely when Adam and Eve disobeyed God in the Garden.

Thankfully, Jesus changes our hearts when we trust in Him, so we can be wise as He is wise. With the Holy Spirit's help, we can grow more like Jesus each day. May His wisdom and love deepen in us and spill over to others!

*Father God, thank You for Your promise of wisdom.
Grant me a deeper knowledge of Your Son so that
I may grow wise in Your ways. Amen.*

Encouragement during Difficult Assignments

Then they answered Joshua, "Whatever you have commanded us we will do, and wherever you send us we will go. Just as we fully obeyed Moses, so we will obey you. Only may the LORD your God be with you as he was with Moses. Whoever rebels against your word and does not obey it, whatever you may command them, will be put to death. Only be strong and courageous!"
JOSHUA 1:16–18 NIV

God gives us difficult assignments just as He did with Joshua. We *know* God will bless us if we're faithful, but we don't always *feel* it. Often the job seems bigger than our capabilities, and we get discouraged. But God wants us to *know* and *feel* He is responsible for the outcome. We just need to be faithful to act.

As with Joshua, God brings people into our lives to encourage us. The men in today's verses encourage Joshua in four ways: they assure him of their allegiance and willingness to help, they pray for him, they take their own responsibilities seriously, and they offer Joshua words of encouragement he has heard before.

Our assignment is for our benefit and to benefit those around us. While we need to be obedient to do the next right step, we also need to encourage others around us. How can you use one of those four ways to encourage someone else?

Heavenly Father, thank You for loving us enough to include us in Your work. Bring people into our lives to encourage us on the journey, and open our eyes to see others who need encouragement. Amen.

The Reward of Faith

"So on that day Moses swore to me, 'The land on
which your feet have walked will be your inheritance
and that of your children forever, because you have
followed the Lord my God wholeheartedly.'"
Joshua 14:9 niv

If we look back on the story of Caleb in Numbers 13 and 14, we see that his heart overflowed with confidence in God. If God said Israel was supposed to get the land, then it didn't matter who was living there; the Israelites would defeat them. Caleb believed that God would do what He said He would do. He was enthusiastically optimistic.

The Anakites, the giants Caleb and Joshua originally spied over forty years earlier, still controlled the land Caleb was to inherit. And he was eighty-five years old. But he was not ready for retirement. He had followed God wholeheartedly, the key to his effectiveness. He was filled with the presence and the power of God. He had pursued God, like a hunter closing the gap on his prey. Caleb still welcomed a challenge. Caleb believed God still had work for him to do and would give him the strength to remove the giants from his land.

Ultimately, this is God's story, not Caleb's. Caleb just applied the principle of sowing and reaping, and God showed up like He said He would. Like Caleb, we can rely on God's strength and power to work through us even if we have physical and mental limitations.

Heavenly Father, thank You for always showing up, bigger and
better than we expect. Show us where we need to trust You. Amen.

A Day Like That

*When you were dead in your sins and in the uncircumcision
of your flesh, God made you alive with Christ. He forgave
us all our sins, having canceled the charge of our legal
indebtedness, which stood against us and condemned
us; he has taken it away, nailing it to the cross.*
COLOSSIANS 2:13–14 NIV

Have you ever had a day that felt doomed for dismal right out of the gate? No, forget the gate; you didn't make it that far. It was right out of the warm blankets that you didn't want to leave.

The demands of the day were firmly in place, and they beckoned you out into a much colder space, sometimes quite literally. You took no time to pause with God. "Took time?" you say. There was no time. Your attitude suffered miserably in the trenches of your duties. Yes, now you are in the trenches.

There (in the trenches), other people are quite miserable as well, and you all say and do miserable things. You offend people. They offend you. You forgot for a while what God did for you—redeeming you on the cross.

Now you come to God asking again for His forgiveness, and you forgive the other people from that miserable day.

Have you ever had a day like that?

---

*Lord, thank You for placing our sins on
the cross and redeeming us. Thank You
for your forgiveness and love. Amen.*

Music to His Ears

Speaking to one another with psalms, hymns, and songs from the Spirit. Sing and make music from your heart to the Lord.
EPHESIANS 5:19 NIV

One of the most powerful moments in the Christian life may turn out to be at a supper table with fellow believers or conversations around a fire. Uplifting and encouraging one another can also happen when we sing. Today many churches resound with praise music which fills the congregation with enthusiasm. These songs should not be directed to those around us but in our hearts to the Lord. Spiritual fullness comes to expression in joyful fellowship, in song and thanksgiving.

King David crawled in caves and crevasses hiding from his enemies, yet he found time to pen many praise songs to the King of kings. Despite his circumstances, he knew God was in control. Paul sang in the dank darkness of a dungeon cell, praising his Creator even though life looked bleak. God's grace was extended to these men as they praised in their suffering.

How much more should we make a melody to the Lord when we are free to move about, to worship, to sing. God wants to hear music from our hearts, not arias with perfect notes. So we will lift up our voices and join in the praise to our Creator and Lord. Harmonious, harsh, or hoarse, He's filtering our melodies with His love.

*Dear heavenly Father, I worship You. I adore You.
Thank You for Your goodness and mercy. Amen.*

Reflecting the Goodness of God

For if you listen to the word and don't obey, it is like glancing at your face in a mirror. You see yourself, walk away, and forget what you look like.
JAMES 1:23–24 NLT

Are you real? There are many reasons people wear masks and refuse to become completely transparent even with those they consider their closest friends.

It's so wonderful to find people who can be real with us. We are drawn to them because they are genuine and true—never pretending. Such boldness and confidence comes with knowing who we are in Christ. As we trust Him to help us, we examine our lives and then learn to shape them to reflect the goodness of God.

It is a process. We begin by looking into the mirror to see what we need to remove of the old person we used to be, so that we can take on the character and nature of God.

Too often, we miss the value of sharing our failings. We don't want to be vulnerable, so we hold back. In doing so, we deprive others of who God created each of us to be. When you share from your own experience—especially your failures—you increase empathy, you're more approachable, and you increase your "relatability" to others. Let your guard down and be all you were created to be.

Lord, help me to be real with those You have put around me. I pray that they see You through me and it draws them closer to You. Amen.

Love and Assurance

*Little children, let us not love with word or with tongue,
but in deed and truth. We will know by this that we
are of the truth, and will assure our heart before
Him in whatever our heart condemns us; for God is
greater than our heart and knows all things.*

1 John 3:18–20 nasb

These verses start out with an admonition—you ought to show your love in what you do. Love is not well expressed by superficial, noncommittal statements. Rather, a true, earnest love will drive you to action. Think about those around you to whom you can express love, not just by telling them, but by showing your love to them in your deeds. Don't allow laziness or excuses to keep you from reaching out to those who need love.

These verses end with a wonderful assurance for those of us who struggle with guilt and fear. When you are in Christ, be encouraged that nothing can take away your salvation. Your heart may condemn you when you fall into the same pattern of sin again or when you fail to do what you promised yourself and God you would do. But be encouraged—you are not in charge of your standing before God. God is. He is greater than any guilt-ridden and self-abasing heart. Once you are one of His children, you will always have that status. He knows all things, including the fact that your name is written, irrevocably, in the book of life.

*Lord, help me to show love, not only in what I say,
but even more so in what I do. Thank You that
You are greater than the fears of my heart.*

Content in Christ's Strength

I have learned how to be content with whatever I have. . . .
I can do everything through Christ, who gives me strength.
PHILIPPIANS 4:11, 13 NLT

Sometimes Paul seems like a giant of a man, way above everyone else on the spiritual scale. Granted, it is a man-made scale, certainly not one God uses.

Paul wrote his letter to the Philippian church from a prison in Rome. Prisons in the ancient world were nothing compared with those in our country today. In chapter one, we learn that Paul was guarded day and night by the emperor's own elite guards—the praetorians. Because Paul never backed down from sharing the gospel with whoever crossed his path, many among the guards believed in Christ and then carried the gospel into Nero's palace. Because of this unique opportunity to spread the gospel, Paul rejoiced.

In the latter part of the letter he declared that the gift the Philippians sent him was welcomed with rejoicing. But even without it he could rejoice because he had learned to be content in whatever situation and condition he found himself. So how was Paul able to do this when so many of God's people today never learn his secret? Before Paul ended the paragraph, he told us: "I can do everything through Christ who gives me strength." Paul couldn't generate contentment in all situations, but Christ in him could. The same "secret" enables God's people to do the same nearly two thousand years later.

Father, thank You for enabling us to live joyful,
contented lives through Jesus Christ.

God's Love

*For I am convinced that neither death, nor life, nor angels,
nor principalities, nor things present, nor things to
come, nor powers, nor height, nor depth, nor any other
created thing, will be able to separate us from the
love of God, which is in Christ Jesus our Lord.*
ROMANS 8:38–39 NASB

In this life we often feel we need to work for love. Love can grow stale or be lost altogether or given to another. The promise of love can be used as a weapon against us. But in this verse, an eternal, genuine love is promised to you. This promise can be trusted because the love of God has been secured through the sacrifice and death of Christ. This is no promise made on a whim or as a manipulation but one made in blood by the perfect Lamb.

No natural or supernatural power can separate you from God's love. Nothing that is currently happening in your life will separate you from God's love. No matter how scary or uncertain the future seems, it will not separate you from God's love. No height of success or depth of depression and despair will separate you from God's love. Nothing that this life and those in it can throw at you and nothing that you do will separate you from God's love. Not even death, which separates us from everything else we know, will separate you from God's love.

Therefore, go forward in peace and boldness, knowing that you are eternally secure and eternally loved.

*Lord, I can't comprehend this kind of everlasting love, but I thank
You that I can rest in the promise that You will always love me.*

His Love Never Quits

Oh, give thanks to the LORD, for He is good! For His mercy endures forever. And say, "Save us, O God of our salvation; gather us together, and deliver us from the Gentiles, to give thanks to Your holy name, to triumph in Your praise." Blessed be the LORD God of Israel from everlasting to everlasting!
1 CHRONICLES 16:34–36 NKJV

God's Word tells us in Psalm 139 that we can never escape the presence of God. He is with us always, no matter where we go or what we do. His love never quits on us. First John 4:10 (NIV) says, "This is love: not that we loved God, but that he loved us and sent his Son as an atoning sacrifice for our sins." God doesn't love us because we did a lot of good things for Him. He doesn't love us because of our last names or because of the jobs we do. He can't love us any more or any less than He already does. He loves us simply because He is our Father and our Creator. In fact, He gave up His very life to show you how much.

You may have had a parent, friend, or husband abandon you at some point in your life. God won't do that. You may feel alone and fearful. God won't leave you. You may feel sad and crushed. God says He is close to the brokenhearted and saves those who are crushed in spirit (see Psalm 34:18).

God, please remove me from godless places of darkness and loneliness and fear. I trust that You love me and that You will be with me always. Amen.

Please God

For God is pleased with you when
you do what you know is right.
1 PETER 2:19 NLT

Few moms hear comments from their children or husband like, "Hey, thanks for washing my basketball uniform," or "I appreciate the way you remind me to do my homework," or "Wow, the toilet bowl is sparkling clean!" Face it. Women just don't receive that kind of encouragement; yet we do those things anyway, with no thought of receiving credit. It's simply what we do for our families.

The same is true as believers. It's always right to do right. Christians serve, give, pray, encourage, and bless others because it is the right thing to do. These actions are as natural to the true believer as escorting a five-year-old across the street is to a mother.

Are you discouraged when no one notices how well you conducted a Bible study or served a church dinner? Does it bother you if your good deeds go unnoticed? Then it's time for a motive-check. God, who knows the thoughts and intents of our hearts, is well pleased when we do what is right, whether or not anyone notices.

We serve without applause because we love God, not because we desire to please men. Besides, the only one we should strive to satisfy is our God, who sees what we do in secret and is well pleased.

Dear Lord, thank You for the encouragement
You give me daily. Although I don't deserve it,
I appreciate Your appreciation! Amen.

Like Glue

*Surely your goodness and love will
follow me all the days of my life.*
Psalm 23:6 niv

Sometimes it's scary to look out into the great unknown. As we stand on the threshold of a new year, we don't know what to expect. Will good things be in store, or do terrible things await?

We don't have the ability to see the future. But we do know one thing for certain. As long as we remain close to our Father, His goodness and love will stay close to us. No matter where we go, no matter where our circumstances may force us, His love and goodness will follow us.

Even when we wander away from His perfect plan for us, He is only a breath away. He promised in Romans 8 that nothing will ever separate us from that love. When life is good, He is there. When life is hard, His love and goodness are right there. Nothing—no sickness or disease, no foul circumstance, no financial difficulty—will remove His love from us. It sticks like glue.

The challenge lies in finding His presence in tough situations. Sometimes we may have to look a little closer or search some odd places. But these things will never change: He is there. He loves us. He is good. And He will never leave us.

*Dear Father, thank You for sticking with me,
no matter what. That knowledge gives me confidence
to move into whatever the future holds. Amen.*

God's Promises

*"God is not human, that he should lie, not a human
being, that he should change his mind. Does he speak
and then not act? Does he promise and not fulfill?"*
NUMBERS 23:19 NIV

Our opinions of God are often shaped by our experiences with people. When we've been hurt, we see God as hurtful. When people lie to us, we subconsciously think of God as a liar. After all, if humans are created in His image, it only stands to reason that God would be like the people in our lives. Right?

Well, no. Yes, we were created in God's image. But we humans are a fallen, broken race. We're sinful. God is without sin.

Humans lie. God doesn't.

Humans go back on their word. God doesn't.

Humans can be mean and hurtful. God is love, and He only acts in love.

God promised good things to those who love Him, those who live and act according to His will. That doesn't mean others won't hurt us or that we won't experience the effects of living in a sin-infested world. But where there's pain, we have a healer. Where there's brokenness, we have a comforter. And where we feel alone, we know we have a friend.

And one day we'll experience the perfect fulfillment of all His promises without the burdens of this world to weigh us down.

Now that's something to look forward to.

*Dear Father, thank You for Your promises. When I feel
discouraged, help me to remember those promises. Amen.*

Knowing God

*Whoever does not love does not
know God, because God is love.*
1 John 4:8 niv

At first glance, this is one of those sweet, easy verses. God is love. And we like to think about love. It's soft and cushy, like velvet.

Yet, if we want full access to that great love of God, we must love others the way He loves us.

Ouch.

If love is patient, then we must show patience to others, or we don't really know God. If love is kind, we too must be kind, or we can't claim a close relationship with God. If love always hopes, always protects, always endures. . .we must do all those things for others, or we can't know God intimately.

We can't be jealous of others, for love is never jealous.

We can't be easily angered, or brag, or dishonor others, or gossip, or seek to elevate ourselves above those around us, because none of those things are characteristic of God's kind of love.

If we want to know God intimately, if we want to experience the rewards of His great love for us, we must allow Him to live out that love in our lives. When we do, we experience a closeness with God that brings our spirits to that soft, velvety place that can only be found in His love.

*Dear Father, I want to know You. I want to love like You
love, so that others can experience Your great love. Amen.*

Fear Not; He Is Peace

"You will keep him in perfect peace, whose mind
is stayed on You, because he trusts in You."
Isaiah 26:3 NKJV

What are you afraid of? Spiders, darkness, cancer, being alone? All the above?

Every human being has fears. Most of us are smarter than to deny that we have any. Bravery has been defined not as a lack of fear but as action in spite of fear. Anyone who has worn a uniform that put her on the front lines of battle whether in the jungle, desert, or city streets understands this principle.

But Jesus promised us more help than simply bluffing our way through the things that frighten us. He gave us the promise of peace. In John 14:27 (KJV), He said, "My peace I give unto you." This heavenly peace keeps our hearts and minds and gives us the strength to do things we never thought we could.

As we leave childhood behind and enter the multifaceted world of adulthood, our fears increase in proportion to our understanding of the world and the things that can go wrong. But the peace that He gives also multiplies to more than fit whatever need we have. And Satan has no fiery dart that can penetrate it.

Lord, thank You for Your peace. Keep my
heart and mind through Christ Jesus. Amen.

Boldly We Come

*God's free gift leads to our being made right with
God, even though we are guilty of many sins.*
ROMANS 5:16 NLT

Why do you think it is that as a general population of people, we often assume that God is out to get us? We tend to jump immediately to the notion that God is angry with us and ready to bring down the hammer. We become afraid to go to church or read the Bible—thinking that as soon as we enter the building or crack the cover, we will drown in waves of guilt and condemnation.

We even become too afraid to pray.

This must be one of the devil's most effective schemes—to convince us to fear talking with God—when talking with God is what will ultimately transform us from the inside out. Indeed, prayer is what we were created for. We were created for a relationship with Him—the entire Bible is the story of our being restored to that relationship.

The next time you are afraid to pray, refuse the fear. Know in confidence that, unlike the devil, you are covered by the blood of the Lamb and can enter freely into His presence. You can enter freely because He chose to open the way to you.

*I will enter into Your presence and sit and talk with
You. I can feel You restore my soul, because this is what
I was made for. This is what I've been missing.*

He Is More Than Able

*Now all glory to God, who is able, through his mighty power
at work within us, to accomplish infinitely more than we
might ask or think. Glory to him in the church and in Christ
Jesus through all generations forever and ever! Amen.*

Ephesians 3:20–21 nlt

Did you ever hear the saying "The more you know, the more it is you know you don't know"? It's true. Whether it's bees or poetry or chemistry or space, the more we learn about a subject, the more we discover how much more there is to know. But while there is ultimately an end to man's knowledge of earthly things, it's impossible to even begin to grasp how big God is. We don't know even a fraction of His power. Our minds are just not capable of fully comprehending His ability, His character, and His love for us.

When we think of God, we tend to think about His abilities relative to our own. We don't even consider doing great things for Him, because we can't fathom how it could happen. Could you be unknowingly limiting God? Whether or not we recognize it, His mighty power, the Holy Spirit, is at work within us, doing more than we can imagine. Avail yourself of this power—let Him do through you things that you can't even begin to comprehend.

---

*Father, You are too big for me. I cannot even begin to comprehend
Your majesty. Thank You for the Holy Spirit, working in and
through me, to accomplish Your purposes through Christ and the
church. Help me to cooperate with Your Spirit's work. Amen.*

Pray without Ceasing

Pray without ceasing. In every thing give thanks:
for this is the will of God in Christ Jesus concerning you.
1 THESSALONIANS 5:17–18 KJV

Pray without ceasing. Pray continually. Never stop praying. Pray all the time.
Regardless of which translation of the Bible you choose, the command is
the same. It seems impossible! How can one pray all the time? Consider
this. You are young and in love. You must go to school and work. You
may be separated by a great distance from your beloved. And yet, every
moment of every day, that person is on your mind. You talk on the phone
and text constantly. His name is always on your lips. So much so that
some of your friends find it annoying! Is your relationship with Jesus like
the one described here? He wants to be the name on your mind when
you are daydreaming. He wants to be the first one you chat with each
morning and the last one you confide in each night. He wants you to be
so utterly absorbed in Him that it begins to annoy some of your friends!
Pray without ceasing. Love Jesus with all your heart. He is crazy about you.

Jesus, thank you that, even in my sin, you died
for me. May my walk with you be the most
important thing in my life. Amen.

Running the Race

Wherefore seeing we also are compassed about with so great a cloud of witnesses, let us lay aside every weight, and the sin which doth so easily beset us, and let us run with patience the race that is set before us, looking unto Jesus the author and finisher of our faith.
HEBREWS 12:1–2 KJV

The Christian life is a race. It must be run with endurance. It requires training and discipline. It is about putting one foot in front of the other, sometimes quickly, sometimes slowly, but always, always moving forward. When a runner stumbles in a 5K or marathon, what does he do? Does he just sit down right then and there and call it quits? If the race is not run with perfection, does he just throw in the towel? Of course not! Likewise, as you are running the race, when you get sidetracked or distracted, when you fall to temptation or take your eyes off the goal, ask Jesus to get you back on track. An old hymn puts it like this: "Turn your eyes upon Jesus. Look full in His wonderful face. And the things of earth will grow strangely dim, in the light of His glory and grace!" Look to Christ, the author and finisher of your faith. He will run right alongside you, encouraging you every step of the way.

*Jesus, help me to keep my focus on You as I
journey through this life. It is not always easy,
but You are always with me. Amen.*

Harmony in Love

Love from the center of who you are; don't fake it. Run for dear life from evil; hold on for dear life to good. Be good friends who love deeply; practice playing second fiddle.
ROMANS 12:9–10 MSG

The call to love in Romans 12:9–10 is extremely difficult to put into practice. Sure, it's easy to love friends and family, but how easy is it to love that person at school or at work when you just cannot relate to her on any level? Being polite is one thing, but truly loving that person is much harder.

Paul tells us that we should not fake love. God says we sin against Him when we *pretend* to love others but dislike them. Instead we are called to *genuine* love. We must be good friends to everyone—the kind of friends who love deeply, from the center of our beings.

The Message uses the metaphor, "practice playing second fiddle," to help us understand how we are to honor one another. In a musical ensemble, the first fiddle typically plays the melody and all the fancy runs. The second fiddle performs the supporting role, harmonizing with the first fiddle, and acting as the musical anchor. We should always take the second part, putting others before ourselves and encouraging them with all our love and devotion. When we love without hypocrisy and honor others above ourselves, we will live in beautiful harmony with one another.

Dear Lord, please help me to love with a genuine heart and to take second place to those around me. Amen.

Simple yet Powerful Words

*Humble yourselves, therefore, under God's mighty
hand, that he may lift you up in due time.*
1 PETER 5:6 NIV

How can a person talk and talk and talk and yet when it comes time to speak words that have great importance, they are speechless? Two of those weighty words are "I'm sorry."

Without those words—and the sincerity of spirit backing them up—marriages fail, friendships break apart, family members suffer, working relationships become strained, and the church loses its ability to minister to people.

So why do we become tongue-tied on those simple words? Because it is easy to justify our position on any matter. Easy to take our own side in an argument. You name it, and we can find a way to point to someone else as the villain in any given circumstance. We must be the heroes, after all. We know our Bibles. We sit in the same pew every Sunday. We can spot sin in someone else's life faster than you can say, "Judgment Day!" But the truth is, sometimes even as Christians, we choose to play the villain in our life story. We forget kindness. We turn our head on justice. We forget the most important scriptures on love.

We need to take a deep look in the mirror, spiritually speaking, asking the Lord to show us if we are at fault and to give us the courage to make things right with others—to say the simple yet powerful words that can change a heart, a life.

*Lord, please give me a humble heart so
that I may always please You. Amen.*

139

Be of Good Cheer

*But the L**ORD** said to Samuel, "Do not consider his appearance or his height, for I have rejected him. The L**ORD** does not look at the things people look at. People look at the outward appearance, but the L**ORD** looks at the heart."*

1 SAMUEL 16:7 NIV

Many are waiting to hear from others that they are valuable. They go from group to group until they settle on the highest bidder. No matter how badly this group mistreats them they think, *This is what I am worth.* But that's not truth. Only God knows your potential. Only God knows the hidden talents He has placed within you. Only God knows His plan for you. Only God knows your heart. Other people will always sell you short!

God told the prophet Samuel to pick out the new king of Israel, for God had revealed he would come from that lineage. Samuel looked over the ones who arrived and asked Jesse if he had another. God was after someone whose heart was turned toward Him. When the youngest, least likely boy arrived, the Lord said, "Rise and anoint him; this is the one" (1 Samuel 16:12 NIV).

David became the king of Israel because he listened to God and poured out his heart to Him. God chose David because God looked at David's heart. And He liked what He saw. Today, turn your heart toward God so He will be pleased.

Father, I choose You this day. Amen.

Kindness

*"Here is my servant, whom I uphold,
my chosen one in whom I delight."*
ISAIAH 42:1 NIV

Jackie and her daughters celebrated Advent in a unique way. They decided that every day they would perform little acts of kindness. They wrote their ideas down, and with much excitement they planned to surprise friends, family, and strangers with unexpected blessings. They paid parking meters that were about to expire, sang carols at nursing homes, gave hot chocolate to the mail carrier, babysat for free, and did many other things anonymously or expecting nothing in return. The result? They were blessed with smiles, thank-yous, and even a few happy tears; and they hoped that their acts of kindness would prompt others to do the same.

In 1 Peter 5:2 (NIV), the Bible says, "Be shepherds of God's flock that is under your care, watching over them—not because you must, but because you are willing, as God wants you to be; not pursuing dishonest gain, but eager to serve."

God calls His people to serve, and service comes in many forms. Some work actively in the church as ministers and missionaries. Others volunteer in their communities through homeless shelters, fund-raising projects, food banks, and other causes. And every day, Christians like Jackie and her girls work silently in the background performing little acts of kindness.

Can you encourage someone today through a little act of kindness?

*Dear God, how can I serve You today?
What can I do to show kindness to others? Amen.*

Different Kinds of Love

*This is my commandment, That ye
love one another, as I have loved you.*
JOHN 15:12 KJV

Not all love is the same according to the Greek translation of God's Word. For instance, *philia* is defined as a loyalty and friendship for family members or friends. *Eros* is a passionate, sensual desire. *Storge* is a natural affection shown between parent and child.

The one most familiar comes from the word *agape*, meaning not only general affection but to hold someone in high regard. The New Testament applies agape love in the relationship between Jesus and His disciples. It is one of self-sacrifice and a giving spirit to all, both friend and foe.

Jesus commands us to love our neighbor as we love ourselves (Matthew 22:39). He doesn't say, "Love your neighbor as long as they keep their dogs from barking or if they maintain their yard and stay on their side of the fence." Rather, He commands us to love as He loves us.

That's God's agape love. It's unconditional and powerful. Agape love builds not destroys; it accepts others' imperfections and is tolerant of people who do things differently than we do.

What's your definition of love? Take some time today and exercise God's love in the same manner He loves you, and see what happens!

---

*Lord, thank You for loving me unconditionally with all of
my faults and flaws. Help me to love as I am loved. Amen.*

Known and Loved

I am the good shepherd, and I know My own and My
own know Me, even as the Father knows Me and I
know the Father; and I lay down My life for the sheep.
JOHN 10:14–15 NASB

Do you fear being known and rejected? Do you feel that if someone truly knew you they couldn't possibly love you? In these verses, Christ asserts that He knows you. But He doesn't just know you as a casual acquaintance or even an intimate friend. His knowledge runs deeper than that. He knows you in the same way that He knows the Father. In the Trinity, Christ and the Father are one. So He is saying that He knows you in the same way that He knows Himself. There could not be a deeper or more intimate knowledge. He knows all the things that you hide from everyone else—He knows the temptations, the frustrations, the lost hopes, the rejections, the insecurities, and the deep desires that you may hardly acknowledge to yourself.

Even though Christ knows the darkest and most secret parts of you, He still loves you. He doesn't love you because He can gain something from it. He doesn't love you on a surface, nonchalant level. He *laid down His life* for you. There is no greater love. He knows you better than anyone else does, and yet He loves you with a deeper, purer love than anyone else can give you. You are deeply known and deeply loved.

Lord, I can't comprehend that You would love me in spite of all
my faults. Thank You for bestowing on me a love I don't deserve.

Moving in God's Strength

I am full of power by the Spirit of the LORD. . . .
In God I have put my trust; I will not be afraid. . . . I am
for peace. . . . My help comes from the LORD, who made
heaven and earth. . . . Because You have been my help,
therefore in the shadow of Your wings I will rejoice. . . .
Now therefore, O God, strengthen my hands.
MICAH 3:8; PSALM 56:11; 120:7; 121:2; 63:7; NEHEMIAH 6:9 NKJV

At times, when a task lies before us, we begin to doubt our ability. Writers hesitate, their hands hovering above the keyboard. Mothers look at their to-do lists, the words blurring before them as overwhelmed feelings creep in. Businesswomen consider the meeting they will soon be leading, not sure of the words to say. Unfocused, unsure, untethered around the tasks before us, we flounder.

Let God take over. Tap into His power and claim it for yourself. Put all your trust in the God who vanquishes fear, who can help you do all He has called you to do. He's done so in the past, and He will definitely do so in the present. Rejoice in His presence, and allow Him to work through you as your hands begin moving in His strength.

Lord, truly I am full of power by Your Spirit. Trusting You,
I will not be afraid but be at peace because You are my help.
As I rejoice in You, I feel Your energy move through me,
Your strength moving my hands. And I begin. . . .

Secret Desires

Trust in the LORD, and do good; dwell in the land, and feed on His faithfulness. Delight yourself also in the LORD, and He shall give you the desires of your heart. Commit your way to the LORD, trust also in Him, and He shall bring it to pass.

PSALM 37:3–5 NKJV

Some of us never pursue our deepest desires out of fear of what people will think or fear of failure. But such fears can keep us from living the life we long for. So how do we slay the dream killers? We lean on God and become confident in Him. We do things His way. It is then we find ourselves dwelling in His territory and being fed on His promises. Such faithfulness sustains us in a way worldly fears cannot. And when we take joy in God's presence, allowing Him to be our guide and giving all our secret plans and dreams over to Him, He will give us the desires of our hearts. So put all your faith in God, the dream maker. Bring your desires before Him. Listen for every whisper, every leading He sends your way. Then simply trust as you commit your way to Him, not forcing the issue but confident that in His will, His way, His timing, He'll bring all your dreams into being.

Lord, I sometimes hesitate to tell You what my soul really craves. But I know that You alone can satisfy my longings, can make my dreams come true. So, as I delight in You, lead me in the way You would have me go. I am putting all my hope in You. Amen.

Perfect Peace

You will keep in perfect peace all who trust in you,
all whose thoughts are fixed on you! Trust in the LORD
always, for the LORD GOD is the eternal Rock.
ISAIAH 26:3–4 NLT

Our lives are a series of moments. And that's what our minds get caught up in, the day-to-day minutiae, the little niggling worries, the what-ifs, the how-comes, and the why-fors. But God wants us to have a different perspective, not an in-the-moment viewpoint but an eternal one. Because when we look at the big picture, our day-to-day worries—the ones that get our hearts beating out of control and our thoughts ricocheting around in our heads—are really nothing to be upset about. That takes trust in a power so much higher than ourselves. But when we have that trust, that confidence in the eternal Rock who can never be moved, we are blessed with a peace that blesses us within, keeping us healthy in mind, body, spirit, soul, and heart. Such a calm also blesses those around us, for it's contagious.

So fix your mind on the one who sees and knows so much more than you ever will. Put your confidence in the one who has your name written on the palm of His hand. Practice being in His presence during quiet hours. And then, the moment stress and chaos begin creeping in, call God to mind, and He will surround you with that big-picture, perfect peace.

I need Your perfect peace, God. You are my eternal Rock.
Take me out of the present and into Your presence where
peace will reign and blessings abound. Amen.

Even the Little Things

But be sure to fear the Lord and serve him faithfully with all
your heart; consider what great things he has done for you.
1 Samuel 12:24 NIV

No one likes sweeping dust bunnies out from under the fridge, scrubbing grout, or filing taxes. Sometimes the boss will assign a grueling task, or worse, an extremely tedious one. It's tempting to expend the minimum effort required and get on with the better things in life. This can happen in relationships as well—we manage the minimum amount of closeness and small talk without any real depth or connection.

However, as God's children we are called to a higher standard. Not just to "get things over with," but to do all things to His glory. Practically, this means doing our best in whatever task or goal we pursue, knowing that He is the final inspector of our work, tasks both big and small.

So, should we scurry to scour the oven until the metal squeaks for mercy? No, we don't work out of fear or out of cold duty (though sometimes those are the motives that compel us) but because we desire to please God, knowing how much He loves us. The way we do the "little things" reveals for whom we labor—for us? For our employers, family, or friends? We may benefit from our efforts, but ultimately our work is for our Father.

Father God, You see all of my work. Please forgive
me for when I have complained, and help me do
my best in everything and do it out of joy in You.

Call Me

*"Call on me in the day of trouble; I will
deliver you, and you will honor me."*
PSALM 50:15 NIV

"Call me and we'll do lunch."

"Call me and we'll talk more."

"Call if you need anything."

How many times have we said those words or heard them in return? Those two little words, *call me*, which hold such significance, have become so commonplace we barely think about them.

But when God says He wants us to call Him, He means it. He must lean closer, bending His ear, waiting, longing for the sound of His name coming from our lips. He stands ready to deliver us from our troubles or at least carry us through them safely.

David called on God in his troubles. Some of those troubles were of David's own making, while others were out of his control. It's a good thing God doesn't distinguish between the troubles we deserve and those we don't deserve. As far as He's concerned, we're His children. He loves us, and He wants to help us any way He can.

While He doesn't always choose to fix things with a snap of His fingers, we can be assured that He will see us through to the other side of our troubles by a smoother path than we'd travel without Him. He's waiting to help us. All we have to do is call.

*Dear Father, I'm so glad I can call on
You anytime, with any kind of trouble. Amen.*

Behind the Scenes

Now faith is being sure of what we hope
for and certain of what we do not see.
HEBREWS 11:1 NIV

Movies, theater, or sports productions all require people working behind the scenes. The audience very seldom sees what it takes to bring the final product together. Hours of preparation, planning, and technical assimilation come together before an audience sees a single performance—the outcome of the production company's hard work.

In the same way, your faith works behind the scenes of your life to produce a God-inspired outcome to situations you face. What you see is *not* what you get when you walk by faith.

Be encouraged today that no matter what takes place in the natural—what you see with your eyes—it doesn't have to be the final outcome of your situation. If you've asked God for something, then you can trust that He is working out all the details behind the scenes.

What you see right now, how you feel, is not a picture of what your faith is producing. Your faith is active, and God is busy working to make all things come together and benefit you.

Heavenly Father, what I see today is not what I'm
going to get. Thank You for working behind the scenes
to bring about the very best for my life. Amen.

Stillness Strengthens

Be still, and know that I am God: I will be exalted
among the heathen, I will be exalted in the earth.
PSALM 46:10 KJV

The radio plays in the car. The TV blares in the house. Phones ring in both places. The computer delivers email and instant messages. Text messages beep on a handheld device. Our modern world rarely thrusts quiet upon us. Our society rushes from one thing to the next. For many people stillness and quiet don't happen until they fall asleep.

Yet God says He is known in stillness. In Isaiah 30:15 (KJV), we read, "For thus saith the Lord GOD, the Holy One of Israel; in returning and rest shall ye be saved; in quietness and in confidence shall be your strength: and ye would not." God says stillness is good for us. It is how we come to know Him and gain our strength from Him.

He is the Creator of the universe. He makes each twenty-four-hour day. He rules the sun and the moon, the day and the night. He knows every sparrow that falls to the ground. He never slumbers nor sleeps. We can trust Him with the moments of our lives. We can make time for solitude and trust Him to order our day. We can trust Him to meet us in the pause. He is God, so we can be still.

Father, help me today to be still before You.
Enable me to trust You with the cares of my life.

Money, Money, Money

For the love of money is a root of all kinds of evil.
Some people, eager for money, have wandered from
the faith and pierced themselves with many griefs.
1 Timothy 6:10 NIV

Wealth management. Asset allocation. Financial planning. What is God's perspective on money? Many heroes of the faith were financially independent. Abraham was a wealthy landowner. Joseph was Pharaoh's right-hand man. David lived in an elegant palace. Why, then, did Jesus say it was easier for a camel to go through the eye of a needle than for a rich man to enter the kingdom of God?

Money is not the issue. It's our attitude toward money that Jesus warns about. When we love money, it becomes an idol that dominates our thoughts and actions. We are driven to accumulate more. Compromises are made. Corners are cut. People are trampled. Greed tempts us to make poor business decisions. Hoping to hit that financial home run, we may take foolish risks and lose it all. Loving money also prevents generosity. We become miserly when we cling tightly to our assets, unwilling to let go.

Perhaps these heroes of the faith were blessed financially because they had the ability to put money in its proper perspective. They loved the Lord above anything else. Money never hindered their relationship with Him. Let's strive to follow their example.

Dear Lord, may I have Your perspective regarding
money and may I love You foremost. Amen.

Work as Unto God

Work willingly at whatever you do, as though you were working for the Lord rather than for people.
Colossians 3:23 NLT

Whatever you do today, work as if you are working for the Lord rather than for man. What does that mean? For the employee, it means work as if God is your supervisor. He does see and hear everything you do. When you are tempted to slack off, remember that the Bible warns against idleness. When you are tempted to grumble about your boss, remember that God has put you under this person's authority—at least for this time. For the stay-at-home wife or mother, it means that even changing a diaper or washing dishes can be done for the glory of God. This verse has to do with attitude. Are you working in the right spirit? Work is not a bad thing. God created work. God Himself worked in order to create the earth in six days. And on the seventh, He looked at the work of His hands and He rested. Consider your work a blessing. If you are employed, remember today that many are without jobs. If you are able to stay at home with your children and keep your house, keep in mind that many are not able to do so for one reason or another. Whatever you do, work as if you are working for God.

Lord, help me to remember that I am working for You and not for man. You are my eternal reward. I want to please You in all that I set out to accomplish. Amen.

Revealing and Healing

"Call to Me, and I will answer you, and show you great and mighty things, which you do not know. . . . I will bring [them] health and healing; I will heal them and reveal to them the abundance of peace and truth."
Jeremiah 33:3, 6 NKJV

God again beckons His people to put Him to the test. He wants His daughters to call to Him so that He can answer them. He longs to show them great and mighty things. One of these great and mighty things is healing—both physical and spiritual. Part of healing includes an abundant knowledge and experience of God's peace and truth.

In Jeremiah 33, God told the prophet His plans to restore Jerusalem, to bring the people back from captivity in Babylon and to forgive their rebelliousness. He promised mercy and the coming of a descendant of King David who would be called the Branch of Righteousness and who would rule in joy. Chapter 33 bursts with the beauty of God's grace as it points forward to the great plan of rescue, not just for the Jewish people captured by the Babylonian King Nebuchadnezzar during Jeremiah's time, but to the salvation of creation through Messiah Jesus. God accomplished in Jesus the mightiest of deeds, a plan for redemption which we could never imagine. Through Jesus, God revealed to us, daughters of Eve, peace and truth since He is the Prince of Peace and the Way of truth.

Lord of our righteousness, thank You for the beautiful picture of healing in Jeremiah 33 and for its fulfillment in Jesus. Keep healing! Amen.

Facing Grace and Truth

And the Word became flesh and dwelt among us,
and we beheld His glory, the glory as of the only
begotten of the Father, full of grace and truth.
JOHN 1:14 NKJV

In the life of Jesus, we behold the glory of the Father. The Word became flesh so that we could know God intimately. We see in Jesus what the Father is like. The Incarnation shows us that God is full of grace and truth.

When we belong to Christ and are in Him, we are surrounded by grace and truth. Grace is unmerited favor and approval. Truth is an absolute standard, a definitive answer, or a measuring rule. Grace is the cleansing, rushing water of a river. Truth, the banks holding fast, gives the water its power and force.

What does that mean for us in our daily lives? Truth tests thoughts, ideas, and things we hear and see. It helps us evaluate our culture, face our past, and acknowledge and confess our sins. Facing the truth is necessary for repentance.

We must stop denying and rationalizing, and admit our problem before we can truly turn in a new direction. Having faced the truth, we turn in repentance, and what we find before us is grace. Grace forgives us, saves us, loves us, and accepts us unconditionally. Experiencing this grace frees us to forgive, love, accept, and choose others regardless of their performance.

Father, thank You for giving us the Son,
full of Your grace and truth.

Deep Roots

*"They will be like a tree planted by the water that sends
out its roots by the stream. It does not fear when heat
comes; its leaves are always green. It has no worries in
a year of drought and never fails to bear fruit."*
JEREMIAH 17:8 NIV

Watering your garden doesn't seem difficult, but did you know you can
train a plant to grow incorrectly, just in the way you water it? By pouring
water from the hose for only a few moments at each plant, the root systems become very shallow. They start to seek water from the top of the
soil, and the roots can easily be burned in the summer sun. By using a
soaker hose, the water slowly seeps into the ground, and the plants learn
to push their roots deeper into the soil to get water.

Jeremiah talked about a larger plant, a tree. A tree needs deep roots
to keep it anchored in the ground, providing stability. The roots synthesize water and minerals for nourishment and then help to store those
elements for a later time. Our deep spiritual roots come from reading
God's Word, which provides stability, nourishment, and refreshment.

*Father, I do not want to wither in the sun. Help me to immerse
myself in Your Word. When I do, I strike my spiritual roots deeper
into life-giving soil and drink from Living Water. Help me to
be the fruitful follower of You that I am meant to be. Amen.*

The Gift of Encouragement

We have different gifts. . . . If it is
to encourage, then give encouragement.
ROMANS 12:6, 8 NIV

As a Christian, what is the inward desire of your heart? To witness? To serve? To teach? In the book of Romans, Paul lists the different gifts God gives His children according to His grace. These gifts of grace are inward desires and abilities used to further the kingdom of God. Encouragement is one of those gifts.

Have you ever met someone who seems to have the right thing to say at just the right time? Intuitively, she notices when someone is troubled and proceeds to listen and speak words to uplift and encourage.

Paul spoke of encouraging as a God-given desire to proclaim God's Word in such a way that it touches hearts to move them to receive the gospel. Encouragement is a vital part to witnessing because encouragement is doused with God's love. For the believer, it stimulates our faith to produce a deeper commitment to Christ. It brings hope to the disheartened or defeated soul. It restores hope.

Perhaps you are wondering what "gift" you possess. The Bible promises us that every true believer is endowed with at least one or more spiritual gifts (1 Corinthians 12). How will you know your gift? Ask God, and then follow the desires He places on your heart.

Father, help me tune in to the needs of those around
me so that I might encourage them for the gospel's
sake for Your glory and their good. Amen.

A Heavenly Escort

*"Behold, I am with you and will keep you wherever you go,
and will bring you back to this land; for I will not leave
you until I have done what I have spoken to you."*
GENESIS 28:15 NKJV

The journey into adulthood is marked with milestones: the beginning of a career, the beginning of a family, the beginning of a future. It can be scary to face so many decisions and so many unknowns. It's difficult to put one foot in front of the other on such a winding path, with no way to see what lies at the end.

A young woman once moved across the country to follow a career opportunity. Steeped in fear, she stared out the window of the plane as it began its descent. Silently she begged God for an answer to her most pressing question, "Will I feel Your presence here?" Over the next few years that were full of successes, failures, joys, and disappointments, she realized that He was there, in that foreign land, because she was there.

On our journey, there are two things that we, as children of God, can claim for ourselves: God's presence and His perfect preservation. He will be with us no matter where life takes us, and He will keep us securely in the palm of His hand.

*Heavenly Father, please escort me on my journey. Guide my path
and reveal Your will to me every step of the way. I claim the
promises of Your presence and Your preservation in my life. Amen.*

An Extravagant God

*Return to the LORD your God, for he is merciful and
compassionate, slow to get angry and filled with unfailing love.*
JOEL 2:13 NLT

There are often times when we are exhausted and discouraged and we allow our minds to roam to dark places. Despair and disappointment set in. A woe-is-me attitude prevails within us. How is it possible to rise from the doldrums? How do we continue? We turn our faces toward the Lord God and know He is in control.

Scripture tells of God's mercy and loving-kindness. It speaks out and urges us to come back to God. This doesn't necessarily mean a change of circumstances, but a change of heart. This change is a choice we intentionally make. It's not necessary to be in a church building or a revival when we make this choice. While many changes happen there, ours can be in our closet, our car, or our office. We reach inwardly to the Highest and ask for His mercy. And scripture says He is merciful and full of grace. He hears our prayers.

Focusing on the negative, choosing despair, doesn't bring life. Voluntarily focusing on Jesus will. Praise Him for all your blessings: they are there, look for them. Some might be tiny, others magnificent. But they're all because of our Lord Jesus Christ. He is a most patient God and extravagant in His love.

*O heavenly Father, I praise Your name. You are extravagant
in Your love, and I am grateful for all You've done. Amen.*

A Heart of Faith and Honor

"He lifts the poor from the dust and the needy from the garbage dump. He sets them among princes, placing them in seats of honor. For all the earth is the LORD's, and he has set the world in order."

1 SAMUEL 2:8 NLT

This is just a part of the prayer that Hannah, mother of Samuel, prayed as she left her son to live with Eli the priest and serve the Lord all his life. Samuel was her firstborn, the child she desperately prayed to God for, and she fulfilled her promise and left Samuel in the care of Eli.

Have you ever considered how hard it was for her to pray this prayer of praise to God? She finally had a child, but she was committed to her promise to offer him in service to the Lord. She would not be the one to raise him and experience all of his "firsts" in life. And yet she prayed this prayer that does nothing but honor the Lord. Even if there were moments when she wished she hadn't made such a promise, she praised Him. "My heart rejoices in the LORD! The LORD has made me strong" (1 Samuel 2:1 NLT).

We can learn so much from Hannah in the short space she is written about in 1 Samuel. She honored the Lord above all else and trusted His ways. May God give you a heart of courage that honors Him and strengthens you.

Dear Lord, thank You for hearing my prayers and remembering me in Your faithfulness. May I be like Hannah, who fervently pursued and honored You.

Be Known for Love

Dear friends, let us love one another, for love comes from God.
Everyone who loves has been born of God and knows God.
Whoever does not love does not know God, because God is love.

1 JOHN 4:7–8 NIV

"God is love." It is a verse many remember learning in Sunday school or Vacation Bible School. But what does it mean? God is, by His very nature, love. All that He does is out of a heart overflowing with unconditional love. God's unconditional love surpasses any other that we have ever received or given.

Christians are to be known by our love. Lyrics of a song written many years ago put it this way: "We are one in the Spirit. We are one in the Lord. . . . And they'll know we are Christians by our love." But do they? Do the people within your sphere of influence know that you are a Christian by your love? Or do you blend in with the crowd? Be a vessel of grace and peace. Let love be your trademark, a distinctive sign that you are a believer. You may never know the impact this will have for the kingdom.

What does love look like? It takes all shapes and forms. Some examples might be helping others, going the extra mile, offering words of encouragement, or putting your own ambitions aside in order to put others first.

Father, in my family and in my workplace,
please use me as a vessel of love. Amen.

Only through God

For by thee I have run through a troop:
by my God have I leaped over a wall.
2 Samuel 22:30 kjv

We've all heard stories about people performing seemingly impossible acts of heroism in the face of danger—lifting a car off someone, carrying an injured person for several miles to reach help. Other stories tell how people survive being stranded in a blizzard or walk away from a terrible accident uninjured. How did they do this? Common sense often plays a big part in survival, but today's scripture tells us where our strength comes from. God enabled the writer of this verse to survive the obstacles he faced.

We may never face the tragedies we read about or see on the news, but we deal with adversity every day. A job loss, a bad medical diagnosis, or a child being bullied at school are only a few of the problems faced by people like us every day. How do we handle it? We can deal with the trouble that comes our way through God and His powerful strength. We may not face a troop or have to jump over a wall, but by our God, we can face a financial crisis, divorce, or disease. Take courage today in knowing that God is here for you and you can leap over that wall of adversity.

Father, give me the strength to face life's trouble
and run the race until the finish. Amen.

It's Not About the Dos and Don'ts

Who hath saved us, and called us with an holy calling, not according to our works, but according to his own purpose and grace, which was given us in Christ Jesus before the world began, but is now made manifest by the appearing of our Saviour Jesus Christ, who hath abolished death, and hath brought life and immortality to light through the gospel.
2 TIMOTHY 1:9–10 KJV

More than 600 Jewish laws are derived from the Ten Commandments that God gave Moses. Before Jesus the Messiah came, they had to follow a list of rules in order to live a life that pleased God and assured them of His continued blessing in their lives.

Jesus came to the earth; gave His life; and defeated death, hell, and the grave, so you could choose eternal life. You are not saved because of a list of dos and don'ts you follow. Instead, it's all about surrendering your heart to God. You are His child by His grace. Once forgiven, He doesn't remember your sins.

Our world is moved by conditional love: I will love you if you do this or that. Thankfully that has no place in your relationship with God. His love is unconditional. You don't have to work from a list for God to accept you. His grace has already made you lovable and acceptable to Him. There is nothing you can do to make God love you any more or any less.

Lord Jesus, I surrender my heart to You.
Thank You for the gift of eternal life. Amen.

Trials and Wisdom

Consider it pure joy, my brothers and sisters, whenever you face
trials of many kinds, because you know that the testing of your
faith produces perseverance. Let perseverance finish its work so
that you may be mature and complete, not lacking anything.
If any of you lacks wisdom, you should ask God, who gives
generously to all without finding fault, and it will be given to you.
JAMES 1:2–5 NIV

Trials and troubles are an everyday part of living here in a fallen world. Pastor and author Max Lucado says, "Lower your expectations of earth. This isn't heaven, so don't expect it to be."

Things won't be easy and simple until we get to heaven. So how can we lift our chins and head into tomorrow without succumbing to discouragement? We remember that God is good. We trust His faithfulness. We ask for His presence and peace during each moment. We pray for wisdom and believe that the God who holds the universe in His hands is working every single trial and triumph together for our good and for His glory.

This verse in James tells us that when we lack wisdom we should simply ask God for it! We don't have to face our problems alone. We don't have to worry that God will hold our past mistakes against us. Be encouraged that the Lord will give you wisdom generously without finding fault!

Lord Jesus, please give me wisdom. So many troubles are
weighing me down. Help me give You all my burdens,
and increase my faith and trust in You. Amen.

Commands and Reminders

*Make allowance for each other's faults, and forgive
anyone who offends you. Remember, the Lord
forgave you, so you must forgive others.*
COLOSSIANS 3:13 NLT

Paul gives the Colossians a pretty difficult command: forgive others and bear with each other's faults. Why do we have such a hard time forgiving people? When other people offend or hurt us, it is hard for us not to want to get even or to hurt them back. We want them to suffer as we have suffered and to feel the consequences of their hurtfulness.

Paul wisely includes more than the command to forgive and make allowances, though. He also offers a reminder. The command to forgive would probably be rather ineffective by itself. It's such a difficult one to follow that we might be tempted to give it up as impossible. But Paul's reminder, "the Lord forgave you," is enough to stop us in our tracks. Time after time we hurt God with our flagrant sins. We have caused Him pain with our indifference or downright disobedience—yet He still forgives us our sins. Surely we can forgive others for their offenses when God has forgiven us so much more.

*Dear Lord, please teach me to forgive, and give
me the strength to love others. Thank You for
Your forgiveness for my sins. Amen.*

Pleasant Boundaries

*LORD, you have assigned me my portion and my cup; you have
made my lot secure. The boundary lines have fallen for me
in pleasant places; surely I have a delightful inheritance.*
PSALM 16:5–6 NIV

Granted, they didn't have much notice, but when the angel of God told
Lot and his family to leave Sodom, he wasn't kidding. There was no time
to spare. The instructions were clear: Pack up, leave, don't look back. But
Lot's wife couldn't do it. The temptation to look back on all she had left
behind was too great. She paid for her disobedience with her life.

Obeying God's commands is difficult when we focus on what we're
giving up. His guidelines for living a holy life can seem restrictive and
unfair when we think about all we're leaving behind. However, if we look
back, we miss what's ahead.

God's boundaries may seem restrictive at times, but the truth is
He put them into place because He has our best interests in mind. For
example, sex creates intense emotional attachments. God knows that
emotional attachment without commitment equals heartache, so He
has reserved sex for marriage.

When we only look at what we're missing out on, it's difficult to see
what lies ahead. But you can trust your heavenly Father. His boundaries
provide security and protection, and your future holds great promise
and reward.

*Father, thank You for the boundaries You have placed around
my life. Help me to focus on what I'm gaining rather than
what I'm leaving behind when I choose to obey You.*

Purpose in Creation

*"The Spirit of God has made me, and the
breath of the Almighty gives me life."*
Job 33:4 NASB

Life can often be difficult to understand. When we're hurting or when we've experienced loss, we find it easy to question our existence and purpose.

Job easily might have questioned his reason for living; he experienced a number of hardships in a short span of time. By the thirty-third chapter of the book of Job, he has lost his livestock, his farmhands, his shepherds, his servants, and his sons and daughters, and he is suffering from terrible boils all over his body. His three friends and his wife have suggested that he curse God and die, but Job refuses to do so. Instead, he remembers with praise the God who created him.

When we question our existence on this earth, we question God's most treasured creation. Trials and tribulations are certain to come our way—Jesus has promised us that. But we are also promised faithfulness, and we know that even amid our greatest challenges, God will strengthen us.

When life becomes difficult and we wonder what we are doing, let's remember that God created us and that He breathed life into us. We were made on purpose, *with* a purpose, and no matter how challenging our life becomes, God is there to comfort and sustain us.

*Dear Lord, You have given me life. Let me use this gift
to praise Your name and further Your kingdom. Amen.*

A Loving Friend

A generous person will prosper;
whoever refreshes others will be refreshed.
PROVERBS 11:25 NIV

Are you convinced that you don't have enough friends—or perhaps your friends aren't meeting your needs? Consider what kind of friend you are. The timeworn axiom "To have a friend, be one" rings with truth.

Good friends listen deeply. We all need someone who can share our load and with whom we can be gut-level honest. This type of friend is invaluable when you feel you can't go one more step.

Good friends also mentor gently and lovingly. A friend pushes a friend to take care of herself and not forget her own needs in the midst of career, kids, and church activities. Maybe there is someone you could nudge into a healthier lifestyle or more active spiritual life.

Finally, good friends forgive freely. They don't judge too harshly or take things extremely personally. Instead, they give friends the benefit of the doubt, knowing that no woman is perfect and sometimes people make mistakes. They are thankful for grace-filled friends and try to forgive as God has forgiven them.

Heavenly Father, thank You for friends. Give us the ability
to be forgiving, godly, listening friends—and provide us
with relationships that will help us grow and mature.
Most of all, thank You for the friend we have in Jesus.

The Next Step

Your word is a lamp for my feet, a light on my path.
<small>PSALM 119:105 NIV</small>

Change is unsettling. It doesn't matter who we are—old or young, rich or poor, married or single. Change can be exciting, but it also brings with it the unknown. And that can be a little unnerving.

When we face changes, the path ahead often looks dark and twisted. We squint and strain to see down the road, but we just can't see clearly. But we don't always need to see into the distance. We only need to see the step ahead of us. Then another step. Then another step.

When the path ahead is obscure, we can go to God's Word for guidance. His Word will light our way. Oh, it may not tell us exactly what's coming a year from now, or even a month from now. But if we depend on Him and follow the guidance He's given us, His Word will act as a road map for the step ahead. It will light the pathway at our feet, so we know we're not stepping off a cliff.

When we rely on His Word and follow it consistently, we can trust His goodness. Even when the future is unclear, we can move ahead with confidence, knowing He will lead us to the best place for us, and His goodness and love will stay with us every step of the journey.

My Guide, I will continue to spend time in Your word and follow Your leading my life. Even when I am unsure where this path will lead, I know I can trust You. Amen.

Building Friendships

*A friend loves at all times, and a brother
is born for a time of adversity.*
PROVERBS 17:17 NIV

Today's world isn't designed for friendship. It's too fast paced, with too many demands and too much stress. Oh, we're connected to everyone, all the time, through text messaging and cell phones and social media. But as fun as social media may seem, it robs us of face-to-face time. We're so distracted with everything at once, we find it hard to focus on one thing, one person at a time.

But friendship demands one-on-one, face-to-face time. And although most of us don't feel we have a lot of time to give, we must! We simply must make friendship, and building real flesh-and-blood relationships, a priority.

God created us for relationships. And although a well-timed email or text message may lift us up at times, there's simply no replacement for a real live hug. There's no substitute for a friend sitting beside you in the hospital, holding your hand. And we won't have those things unless we're willing to put aside our high-tech gadgets and invest time in the people around us.

Today, let's make it a point to turn off our cell phones. Let's step away from our computers for a while and have a real conversation with someone. That person may just turn out to be a true friend.

*Dear Father, teach me to be a true friend. Help me to make
friendship a priority and invest in the people around me. Amen.*

God's Light for Our Path

*So the cloud of the LORD was over the tabernacle by
day, and fire was in the cloud by night, in the sight
of all the house of Israel during all their travels.*
EXODUS 40:38 NIV

Have you ever been forced to choose between "good" and "best"? When life presents us with more than one great opportunity, it can be hard to decide what to do. The path we should take depends on many different factors, and the road may not be clear at first.

How do we determine God's will? It's an age-old question, and to be sure, discovering God's choice for us is not easy. But it *is* simple. First, we must pray for God's guidance. He promises to give us wisdom when we ask for it. Second, we need to search His Word and make sure our potential decision lines up with scripture. Third, we should ask for counsel from godly advisors. And fourth, we must search our hearts to see if the opportunity fits well with the personality, talents, and priorities God has given us.

Rest assured, God *will* shine His light on the right path, just as He led the Israelites with a cloud by day and a fire by night. And when it comes, His guidance will be accompanied with peace, joy, and a certainty that we have followed one who has our (and His) best interests at heart.

*Faithful Father, I praise You for Your compassion and concern for
me. Guide me with Your holy light as I seek Your will for my life.*

Light

*"You are my lamp, O LORD; the LORD
turns my darkness into light."*
2 SAMUEL 22:29 NIV

The Bible begins with light. Genesis 1:3 (NIV) says, "And God said, 'Let there be light,' and there was light." It also ends with light. Revelation 22:5 (NIV) says, "There will be no more night. They will not need the light of a lamp or the light of the sun, for the Lord God will give them light."

Unfortunately, there's a lot of darkness in between. War. Murder. Pain. Loss.

Scripture certainly doesn't candy-coat the difficulties of life, but even in the midst of the darkness there are glorious glimpses of His marvelous light. David's sin is forgiven, and he becomes a man after God's own heart. Paul is transformed from a murderer of Christians to a passionate evangelist. Peter denies Christ but later defends Christ to the death. God has the amazing ability to turn even our darkest situations into personal and spiritual victories.

Perhaps you are facing a dark situation right now. Maybe you've suffered loss, suffered a moral failure, or missed a chance to defend your faith. If so, you're not alone—you have a lot of company. When it seems that you're surrounded by darkness, remember that light is both your foundation and your future. Release the situation to His marvelous light and know that He is able to transform it into something more than you could ever dream.

---

*God, You are light. In You there is no darkness at all.
Thank You that Your light illumines even my blackest night.*

A Perfect Fit

You were bought at a price.
1 CORINTHIANS 6:20 NIV

Sometimes life can feel like a huge puzzle, and we're constantly trying to figure out how our piece of life fits into the big picture. We all have a desire to belong to something special—someone important. Surprisingly, we can overlook the most important connection we have: we belong to God.

No matter where you've been or what you've done, God has accepted you. He is all about your future, and that includes spending eternity with Him. He shaped you to the perfect size to fit into His purpose and plan. And no matter what road you take, He has made a place for you. He purchased you with the price of His own Son's life. And He gave you everything you need to be accepted as a joint heir with Jesus.

When it seems others do not want you on their team or you find you're having a hard time fitting in, remember you are part of God's family—born of the household of faith. He created you and formed you to be a perfect fit.

Heavenly Father, thank You for paying the ultimate price
for me to be a part of Your family. When I'm tempted to
feel rejected or unwanted, remind me that I don't have
to look far to find my perfect place in You. Amen.

Without Love

*If I speak in the tongues of men or of angels, but do not have
love, I am only a resounding gong or a clanging cymbal.*
1 CORINTHIANS 13:1 NIV

Without love, all the good deeds in the world are just a bunch of noise!
Like resounding gongs or clanging cymbals, the Pharisees of Jesus' day
went about their good works. Over and over, they repeated them. They
were duties, not desires of the heart. They based everything on ritual
rather than relationship. Are there Pharisees among us today? Certainly!
Our job as Christ-followers is to show the world the love of God. We do
this with open hearts and open arms. We do it in the workplace, in the
marketplace, and in our homes. We do it as we come and go; with our
children and with other people's children; with our spouses, neighbors,
and coworkers. The world desperately needs to see extravagant love in
us, love that cannot be explained by any means other than the fact that
we walk with the author and creator of love. Don't go about your good
deeds out of guilt or so that someone will notice how nice you are. Do
good deeds so that others will notice Jesus in you and glorify your Father
who is in heaven. Do good deeds out of love. It will always come back
to you tenfold.

*Lord Jesus, give me opportunities to love this
world so that others might see You in me. Amen.*

Introducing Jesus

He first found his own brother Simon,
and said to him, "We have found the Messiah"
(which is translated, the Christ).

JOHN 1:41 NKJV

"We have found. . ."These are loaded words. The speaker implies that he has been looking for something. Andrew's words indicate a prior sense of expectation, longing, and watchfulness. There is triumph in his voice, and the first person he tells his good news to is his own brother, Simon. The Bible does not tell us Andrew worried about Simon's reaction. He simply talks about whom he has found. He introduces his brother to Jesus. Beyond that point, Christ takes the initiative. He immediately calls Simon to Himself and changes his name to Peter.

We often make evangelism much more complicated than it has to be. Witnessing is as simple as what Andrew said to Simon Peter: "We have found. . ." How often do we lose sight of what we have found while focusing on another's problem? Jesus is not merely one part of our lives. He is the Messiah, the Christ, and our Savior. We simply need to say, "I found Him"—the simplest way to introduce Him to others. And like He did with Simon Peter, Jesus will take over from there.

Lord Jesus, help me remember the thrill of meeting
You and convey that to others. Show me the things
that have lured me away. Draw me back to the joy
of my salvation, and use that to draw others to You.

Three Strings

*Two people are better than one, because they get more
done by working together. If one falls down, the other
can help him up. But it is bad for the person who is
alone and falls, because no one is there to help. . . .
A rope that is woven of three strings is hard to break.*
ECCLESIASTES 4:9–10, 12 NCV

God uses His people to encourage and strengthen one another. As
iron sharpens iron, so a friend sharpens a friend (Proverbs 27:17). We
get more accomplished in our own lives—and in the grand scheme of
things—when we are open to the help and encouragement of others.

If you see a friend in need of physical, emotional, or spiritual help—
ask the Lord to give you the wisdom and understanding to be used in
helpful ways. And when a friend offers similar help to you, don't be too
proud to accept it.

Ask the Lord to guide you in finding a "three-string" accountability
partner. Look for a Christian woman with a strong faith in the Lord who
is willing to pray with you, encourage you in your faith, and be honest
about your strengths and weaknesses. Meet together several times a
month and ask each other the hard questions: Were you faithful to the
Lord this week? Did you gossip? Is there anything you're struggling with
right now? How can I pray for you?

With God, you, and a trusted Christian friend working together,
you become a rope of three strings that is hard to break!

*Father, thank You for using Your people to encourage and
sharpen me. Guide me as I seek an accountability partner that
will help me grow in my relationship with You. Amen.*

Cheering You On!

If God is for us, who is against us?
ROMANS 8:31 NASB

When others believe in you, they encourage and promote you. You know they're going to lift you up, and it helps you to reach higher for your goals and stand stronger against your opposition. It helps to know that they are supporting you—cheering you on.

Think about a little boy on a baseball team. It's his first year and he's just learning the game, but his coach lets him know he's nothing special. The boy knows his coach doesn't believe in him, and he doesn't have one single good game all year.

The next year he has a new coach who sees potential in all his players. The coach treats the boy like a star. With encouragement from him, the boy performs like the winner his coach sees him to be.

Consider your own support network. Who do you rely on to help you up when you're down or to inspire you to new heights? The Lord is your number one fan. He sees you at your fullest potential, and He's always ready to hold you up. The Bible is a great place to find His encouraging words and instruction. No matter what you're facing, He's cheering you on right now.

---

*Lord, help me to see myself as You see me. I know that
You believe in me, and that brings courage to my
heart. I am determined to reach higher and stand
stronger knowing You are on my side. Amen.*

Working 9 to 5

*For we hear that some among you are leading
an undisciplined life, doing no work at all,
but acting like busybodies.*
2 Thessalonians 3:11 nasb

The job you have now may not be exactly the glamorous career you had in mind. You may struggle with what to do between 9:00 a.m. and 5:00 p.m. Should you actually do all the mundane things your boss wants you accomplish, or should you spend a more pleasant day chatting on the phone, reading magazines, and texting your friends?

It may be difficult to stay on task at a job that's less than rewarding, but God's Word tells us about the importance of living a disciplined life and working hard. Even if you hate your job, ask God to change your attitude about work in general. Instead of considering your work torture, see it as an opportunity to serve the Lord. Work hard and let your actions serve as an example for others. Be cheerful in adversity.

Most of all, try to see your office as a mission field. Instead of chatting on the phone, show the love of Christ to someone at work who needs Him. The most difficult office situation can be turned into an opportunity with a little prayer and dedication.

*Father, it's not always easy to stay focused at my job.
Help me to remember that what I'm doing at
work is all part of my service to You. Amen.*

Juggling It All

*God will make you fit for what he's called you to be,
pray that he'll fill your good ideas and acts of faith with
his own energy so that it all amounts to something.*
2 THESSALONIANS 1:11–12 MSG

Do you feel like your life is a nonstop juggling routine? Maybe some days feel more like a juggling act on an ever-swaying, sometimes-lunging cruise ship. Now that takes a special set of skills!

Most of the time our busy schedules aren't as enjoyable as a juggling routine: maintaining a well-ordered home, endless laundry, career, school, kids, grocery shopping, and don't forget small-group Bible study for fellowship and church to feed the soul. To top it all off, maybe there's a nagging sense of failure you feel that each area is done with less than your best effort.

Know that God will make you fit for each task He's called you to do, giving you the energy you need. What doesn't get done lies in His hands. He'll provide the creativity and resources you need through the times of ever-swaying circumstances.

*God, anchor of my soul, steady me through these
unpredictable times. Help me to balance all You
want me to do. I trust You with the rest. Amen.*

God Knows Your Name

But now, this is what the LORD says—he who created you,
O Jacob, he who formed you, O Israel: "Fear not, for I have
redeemed you; I have summoned you by name; you are mine."
ISAIAH 43:1 NIV

Do you remember the first day of school? The teacher called the roll, and you waited for your name to be announced. When it was, you knew that you were a part of that class—you belonged there.

We wait for our names to be called a lot in life: when captains pick teams, while sitting in a doctor's waiting room, or before being called in for a job interview. There is comfort in hearing our own names, in being recognized.

God knows your name. He created you and redeemed you from sin through His Son, Jesus, if you have accepted Him as your personal Savior. He knows you. He put together your personality and topped off His masterpiece by giving you all sorts of likes and dislikes, dreams and desires, passions and preferences. You are His unique design, His daughter, His beloved one.

No matter if you feel you don't belong, *you belong to God*. He takes great joy in you. You are His treasure. He sent Jesus to die on the cross to give you an abundant life. He wants to spend eternity with you! He calls you by name, and your name is music to your Father's ears.

Lord, I thank You for knowing my name
and loving me unconditionally. Amen.

I Think I Can

"Do not be afraid; only believe."
MARK 5:36 NKJV

A children's story from the 1930s, *The Little Engine That Could,* tells of a small switch engine that is asked to pull a long train up over a high mountain after many larger engines refused the job. Someone had to do it, and the optimistic little engine succeeds by repeating to himself, "I think I can! I think I can!"

Our society is filled with people who tell us we can't do this or that. Maybe you were told not to get your hopes up, yet those who defy the odds become heroes as we see their amazing stories on the news. They refused to be stopped by something that only looked impossible.

Take a trip through the Bible and you'll see that those God asked to do the impossible were ordinary people of their day, yet they demonstrated that they believed God saw something in them that they didn't see. He took ordinary men and women and used them to do extraordinary things.

When you believe you can do something, your faith goes to work. You rise to the challenge, which enables you to go further than before, to do more than you thought possible. Consider trying something new— if you think you can, you can!

God, I want to have high expectations. I want to do more than most think I can do. Help me to reach higher and do more as You lead me. Amen.

Working Together

For we are labourers together with God:
ye are God's husbandry, ye are God's building.
1 CORINTHIANS 3:9 KJV

Isn't it amazing that God allows us to work with Him to accomplish great things for His kingdom? In reality God could have called on His angels to do the jobs He assigns to us. He could have chosen a method to fulfill His work that would have required less dealing with stubbornness and excuses; but God chose to use us—His human creation. What a wonderful privilege we have!

Not only does God choose to use us in His work, He also continues to work in our lives to mold us into the masterpieces He has planned. The more we allow Him to do *in* us, the more He will be able to do *through* us.

It is important to realize that God wants to work in and through us all our lives. We are not complete until we reach heaven, when we will see Christ as He is. If we become satisfied with who we are while yet on earth, it is pride—the beginning of our downfall. The more content we are with our spiritual maturity, the less God can use us. We must strive daily to be more like Christ if we desire to be useful to God.

O great God, it is an honor to serve You. I ask You to
work in my life that I might be useful to Your work.

The-God-Who-Sees

*Now the Angel of the LORD found her. . . . [and] said to
her, "Return to your mistress, and submit yourself under
her hand.". . . Then she called the name of the LORD
who spoke to her, You-Are-the-God-Who-Sees.*
GENESIS 16:7, 9, 13 NKJV

Hagar ran away from her circumstances: Sarai, an abusive mistress. Part of
Hagar's trouble had been caused by her own actions. For having become
pregnant by Abram, she had begun disrespecting the childless Sarai.

We too sometimes think we can run from our troubles. But when we
come to the end of ourselves, God is there, ready to give us the wisdom
we need but may not want. He may ask us to go back, telling us how to
"be" in our circumstances: submissive, obedient, loving. He had a vision for
Hagar that she would be the mother of a son and have many descendants.

Even today, this God-Who-Sees sees you and your situation. He
is ready to reveal Himself to you and share His wisdom. He may not
remove you from your circumstances, but He will give you the word you
need to get through them. Afterward, you'll see your situation in a new
light, with a new hope for your future, step by step.

---

*Lord, You constantly reveal Yourself, manifest Yourself to me. In fact,
You see me before I even come to You. So be with me now. Show me
where You want me to submit. Remind me that You have a plan and
vision for my life—and that it is all meant for my good. Amen.*

With All Your Strength

Whatever your hand finds to do,
do it with all your might.
ECCLESIASTES 9:10 NIV

"Now we have one day more," said Oxford chaplain Joseph Alleine in 1664. "Let us live well, work hard for souls, lay up much treasure in heaven this day, for we have but a few to live." Little did he know that only four years later, at age thirty-four, his time on earth would end.

Every single moment of life is a gift. We dare not waste one. "To live is Christ," said the apostle Paul (Philippians 1:21 KJV). Our lives were made to reflect God's glory, not just on Sundays or mission trips or during women's Bible study class, but in respecting our husbands and modeling decency and kindness for others. It's in the things we say, do, and think when no one is there to give credit. It's in the times we choose to do the right thing, even when it hurts.

Every moment has a purpose for God's kingdom. It's time to be zealous for righteousness in the course of everyday life, and God has promised a treasure trove awaiting us in heaven. The irony is that earthly life will also be filled with treasures—happy marriages, strong children, peace of mind, and joy unspeakable and full of glory.

God, I pray that my passion for You shows
through my daily life. Put a fire in my soul
that burns so bright others can see it. Amen.

Seeking Advice

The LORD says, "I will guide you along the best pathway
for your life. I will advise you and watch over you.
Do not be like a senseless horse or mule that needs
a bit and bridle to keep it under control."
PSALM 32:8–9 NLT

There is a key word in this passage: "advise." The Lord says He will advise us and watch over us. But what if we don't take the time to ask for His guidance? How many times have we been sidetracked, lost, and confused simply because we never asked for the Lord's advice?

In the hurried lives we live, it's easy to fall into a routine and switch over to autopilot. Our calendars are teeming with activities and deadlines, and all too often we simply enter "survival mode." You could say that we become similar to the mule in this scripture—putting hardly any thought into our days and simply being guided by chaos and distraction.

God has more for us. If we take the time to seek out His counsel, He will advise us. He will guide us along the best pathway for our lives and watch over us. He will give us purpose, and our lives will be filled with adventure and divine encounters.

Lord, thank You for opening my eyes to the reality that
You desire to guide my life. Forgive me for being so
busy, and help me to slow down and seek Your counsel.
I want to walk this journey of life with You.

Owning Your Faith

*But the Helper, the Holy Spirit, whom the Father will
send in My name, He will teach you all things, and bring
to your remembrance all things that I said to you.*
JOHN 14:26 NKJV

Is your faith deeper and stronger than when you first accepted Jesus? Or are you stuck back in the early, childish days of your faith?

We each must make our own personal choice to continue to build our faith. Rather than just taking things at face value, we need to wrestle with issues so that we can own God's truths and share them with others. No longer a simple, "Because the Bible says so," it now becomes a matter of, "Where does the Bible say it and why?" Instead of expecting others to lead us, we each need to nurture a personal desire for deepening our relationship with God.

While we are responsible for choosing to grow in faith, we don't do it on our own. Jesus promises that the Holy Spirit will teach and guide us if we allow Him to. He will help us remember the spiritual truths we've learned over the years. Fellowship with other Christians also helps us to mature as we share our passions and are encouraged.

God wants you to own your faith. Make it real with words and actions.

*Jesus, I want to know You intimately. Help me to
mature in my walk with You daily. Guide my
steps as I seek You through Your Word. Amen.*

Scripture Index

OLD TESTAMENT

NEW TESTAMENT